The AMERICAN HERITAGE®

First
Dictionary

By the Editors of the American Heritage® Dictionaries

HOUGHTON MIFFLIN

Boston • New York

Staff

Editorial

Kaethe Ellis
Senior Coordinating Editor

Ann-Marie Imbornoni
Associate Editor

David M. Weeks
Senior Editor

Art and Production

Christopher Leonesio
Production and Manufacturing Manager

Patricia McTiernan
Production Supervisor

Margaret Anne Miles
Senior Art and Production Coordinator

Designed by Textart, Inc., New York

Text design	**Niza Hanany**
Commissioned artwork	**Eva Vagretti Cockrille**
Letter opener photographs	**Ken Karp**
Letter opener artwork	**Michelle Dorman**

American Heritage and the eagle logo are registered trademarks of Forbes Inc. Their use is pursuant to a license agreement with Forbes Inc.

Visit our website: www.houghtonmifflinbooks.com

ISBN 0-618-28007-3

Library of Congress Cataloging-in-Publication Data

The American heritage first dictionary : A to Z / by the editors of
the American heritage dictionaries.
    p. cm.
    Summary: An illustrated reference book including an A to Z
vocabulary listing, a section on "How to Use Your Book" and a
section on phonics.
    ISBN 0-395-85761-9 (hardcover)
    1. English language—Dictionaries, Juvenile. [1. English
language—Dictionaries.]
PE1628.5.A444 1997
423—DC21   96-47325

Manufactured in the United States of America

cover photos: © 2003 PhotoDisc, Inc./Getty Images: balloons; Robertstock.com/Camerique: Dalmatian (front cover and spine); © School Division, Houghton Mifflin Company: xylophone; Stone-Peter Dazeley/Getty Images: pinwheel; The Image Bank-Kevin Morris/Getty Images: scallop; Albano Ballerini: patch (back cover); Animals Animals-Earth Scenes/Margot Conte: paw (back cover)

HOW TO USE YOUR DICTIONARY

What is a Dictionary?

A dictionary is a book about words. The dictionary tells you how to spell a word. The dictionary tells you what a word means. The dictionary shows you how to use a word in a sentence.

How to Find a Word

This dictionary has words in **ABC** order. You have to know the alphabet to find a word in the dictionary. All the words that begin with **A** come before all the words that begin with **B** because **A** comes before **B** in the alphabet. And all the words that begin with **B** come before all the words that begin with **C** because **B** comes before **C** in the alphabet.

A B C D E F G H I J K L M N O P Q R S T U V W X Y Z

a b c d e f g h i j k l m n o p q r s t u v w x y z

Look at the boxes at the top of the dictionary's white pages. Each box has a letter of the alphabet in it. All the words that begin with **A** are on the pages with **A**. All the words that begin with **B** are on the pages with **B**. And all the words that begin with **C**, **D**, **E**, **F** through **Z** are on the pages with **C D E F** and **Z** boxes.

Looking Up a Word

Let's look at the letter **C**. All the words in the dictionary are in ABC order. And all the words that begin with the letter **C** are in ABC order, too. Look at each letter of each word.

came comes before **camel** because **camel** has more letters	c a m e c a m e l
cap comes before **car** because **p** comes before **r** in the alphabet	c a p c a r
carrot comes before **carry** because **o** comes before **y** in the alphabet	c a r r o t c a r r y

Let's look up **caterpillar**. Look for the box with **C**. Find the beginning of the **C** words. Read the **C** words in ABC order until you find **caterpillar**. Where is **caterpillar**? **Caterpillar** comes in the ABC's after **catch** but before **cattle**:

ca**s**tle

ca**t**

ca**tch**

caterpillar

cat**tle**

Caterpillar comes on page 52. The page numbers are at the bottom of the pages. **Caterpillar** and the other words you look up are in big, blue letters.

What You Can Learn About a Word in the Dictionary

What does the dictionary tell you about **caterpillar**?

- The dictionary spells the word.

- The dictionary tells you what the word means.

- The dictionary often gives you a picture of the word.

caterpillar

A **caterpillar** is an insect. It looks like a worm covered with fur. **Caterpillars** change into butterflies or moths.

Sometimes a word will have more than one meaning. If you look up the word **orange,** you can see that it has two meanings.

orange

1. An **orange** is a kind of fruit. It is about the size of a tennis ball. **Oranges** grow on **orange** trees.
2. **Orange** is a color. Pumpkins and oranges are **orange**.

A number comes before each meaning when more than one meaning is given.

Different Forms of Words

Sometimes words have different forms. **Dogs** is the form of the word **dog** that you use when you mean more than one dog. It is usual to add **s** to a word to show more than one. **Plays** and **play** are forms of the word **play** that you use to tell about something happening now.

José **plays** the piano.
Maggie and Michael **play** in the park.

Played is the form you use to tell about something that happened in the past.

Anna **played** basketball yesterday with her brothers.

It is usual to add **s** or **ed** to words to show when something happens. But some words have special forms that are not usual. **Goose** is a word like this because when you mean more than one **goose** you do not say *gooses*, you say **geese**. **Go** is a word like this, too.

We like to **go** to the zoo.
Adam **goes** to the zoo often.
We **went** to the zoo last Saturday.
We have **gone** to the zoo many times.

Goes, **went**, and **gone** are all forms of the word **go**. In the dictionary, special forms of a word are given after the meaning or meanings.

grow

1. To **grow** is to get bigger. Animals and plants **grow** as they get older. **2.** To **grow** up means to become a woman or a man. When you **grow** up, you may be taller than your father. —**grew, grown**

If you look up **grew**, it will tell you that it is a form of **grow**.

grew

Grew is a form of **grow**. Dale **grew** tomatoes in the garden last summer. Sharon always wanted to be a teacher and when she **grew** up that is what she became.

Different Words That Are Spelled Alike

Sometimes two different words with different meanings have the same spelling. The dictionary puts little blue numbers after these words. The numbers are a little above the big, blue words.

bat¹

A **bat** is a thick stick. It is used to hit a ball. **Bats** are made of wood, metal, or plastic.

bat²

A **bat** is a small animal. A **bat** has a body like a mouse and wings. **Bats** sleep during the day and fly around at night.

A B C D E F G H I J K L M N O P Q R S T U V W X Y Z
a b c d e f g h i j k l m n o p q r s t u v w x y z

a

A means one. Red is **a** color. Our friends will stay with us for **a** day or two.

able

Being **able** to do something means that you can do it. If you can run fast enough you will be **able** to win a race.

about

1. The people in this story are Lisa and David. The story is **about** Lisa and David. **2. About** means nearly. That line is **about** four inches long.

above

above

Above means higher. Airplanes fly **above** the ground.

absent

Absent means not here. Two students were **absent** because they were sick.

accident

An **accident** is something you did not want or expect to happen. I broke my glasses by **accident.**

acorn

An **acorn** is a nut that grows into an oak tree.

across

Across means from one side to the other. A bridge was built **across** the river.

acorn

act

To **act** means to behave in some way. Sometimes Tom **acts** like a clown.

actually

Actually means really. Ann didn't think she would like the party, but when she got there, she **actually** had fun.

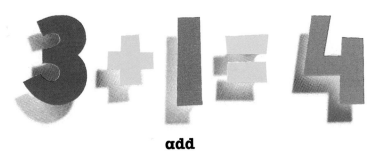

add

add

1. To **add** means to put together. Steve drew a picture of his brother. Then he **added** a funny nose and glasses. **2.** To **add** also means to put numbers together. When you **add** three and one, you get four.

address

An **address** is the name of a place. You put an **address** on a letter to tell the post office where to send it.

Daniel Smith
56 Grove Street
Madison, WI 62371

Sharon Johns
145 Hudson Street
New York, NY 12543

address

afraid

To be **afraid** means to think something bad will happen to you. Some people are **afraid** of the dark.

after

After means following. **After** the ball game, we went home. Steve ran fast when his brother came **after** him.

afternoon

Afternoon is the part of the day between noon and sunset. **Afternoons** are short in winter and long in summer.

again

Again means a second time. Timmy went sailing on Friday. He went **again** on Sunday.

against

against

1. **Against** means on or touching on the side of something. Kathy put her bicycle **against** the wall.
2. To be **against** someone means to try to beat them at a game. Two teams play **against** each other.

age

The **age** of something is how old it is. John is seven years old. He is tall for his **age**.

ago

Ago means in the past. Dinosaurs lived a long time **ago**.

agree

To **agree** means to share the same idea. Sarah and Kate **agreed** to take turns.

air

Air is a gas that people breathe. **Air** is all around us. We cannot see it, but we can feel it when the wind blows.

airplane

airplane

An **airplane** is a machine with wings that flies in the air. **Airplanes** carry people from one place to another.

airport

An **airport** is a place where airplanes take off and land.

alike

Alike means the same. Twins look **alike.**

alive

Alive means living and growing. Animals and plants are **alive** until they die.

all

All means with nothing left out. **All** horses have four legs. Beth ate **all** of her breakfast.

alike

alligator

An **alligator** is a very large reptile.
It has short legs, a long tail, and
strong jaws with sharp teeth.
Alligators live in rivers and
swamps where the weather
is warm.

alligator

almost

Almost means nearly. Marcel's birthday is next week.
He is **almost** six years old.

alone

alone

Alone means by yourself. Maggie likes to be **alone**
in her room.

along

1. **Along** means in a line with. It is nice to walk **along**
the beach. 2. **Along** also means together. Donna went
to the store and her brother went **along** with her.

aloud

Aloud means so that other people can hear. Joan read a story **aloud** to her friends.

alphabet

alphabet

An **alphabet** is the letters that people write with. Our **alphabet** is A, B, C, D, E, F, G, H, I, J, K, L, M, N, O, P, Q, R, S, T, U, V, W, X, Y, Z.

already

Already means before this. Kim missed the bus today. When he got to the bus stop, it had **already** gone.

also

Also shows something added. Laura plays the piano. She can **also** play a trombone.

always

Always means every time. Manuel is never late for school. He **always** comes on time.

am

Am is a form of **be.** It is used with **I.** "Are you six years old?" "No, I **am** seven."

amount

An **amount** is how much there is of something. An elephant needs a large **amount** of food. A mosquito makes a small **amount** of noise.

an

An is a form of **a.** It is used before words that begin with A, E, I, O, or U. A new pen writes better than **an** old one.

anchor

An **anchor** is a heavy object that helps a ship stay in one place. **Anchors** come in many different shapes.

anchor

and

And joins two things together. Three **and** two are five. Bonnie **and** Jane are best friends.

angry

To be **angry** means to feel very upset with someone. Bill's dad was **angry** at him because he broke a window.

animal

An **animal** is anything alive that is not a plant. Dogs, cats, fish, birds, and insects are all **animals.**

another

Another means a second one. Tina ate a carrot. She liked it so much she ate **another** one.

answer

An **answer** is what you give when someone asks a question. The teacher asked a question. Tom knew the right **answer.**

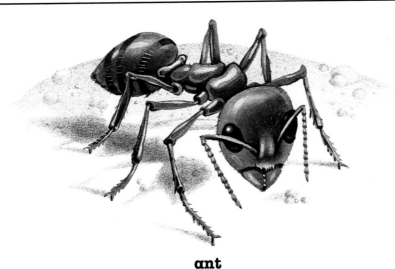
ant

ant
An **ant** is an insect. **Ants** live in large groups in trees or in tunnels in the ground.

any
1. Any means that it does not matter which one. Take **any** seat you like. **2. Any** also means some. Do you want **any** of my sandwich?

anybody
Anybody means any person. Steve didn't know **anybody** at the party.

anyone
Anyone means anybody. Invite **anyone** you like for dinner.

anything
Anything means any thing. My brother will eat **anything**.

anyway
Anyway means that something doesn't matter. Michael's foot hurt, but he tried to walk **anyway**.

anywhere

Anywhere means
in any place. Sit
anywhere you like.

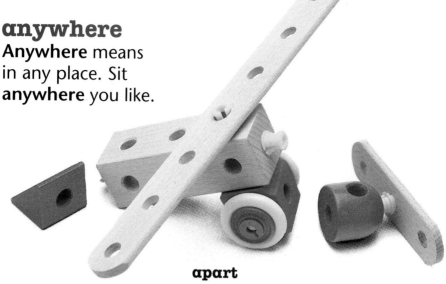

apart

apart

1. Apart means away from each other. A chicken's
toes are far **apart**. **2. Apart** also means in pieces.
Mario likes to take things **apart** to see how they work.

ape

ape

An **ape** is an animal with long arms and no tail.
Apes can stand up straight. They are like humans
in many ways.

apple

apple

An **apple** is a kind of fruit. **Apples** have red, yellow, or green skin.

April

April is a month of the year. It has thirty days. **April** comes after March and before May.

aquarium

An **aquarium** is a glass box or bowl that is filled with water. People who have fish at home keep them in **aquariums.**

aquarium

are

Are is a form of **be.** It is used with **you, we,** and **they.**
"Where can my shoes be?" "They **are** in the closet."

area

An **area** is a space. The kitchen is an **area** where we cook food. An ocean covers a large **area**.

aren't

Aren't is a short way to say **are not**. Bananas **aren't** blue. They are yellow.

arm

An **arm** is a part of the body. It is between the shoulder and the hand. Amy used both **arms** to carry wood for the fireplace.

arm

armor

Armor is a hard shell that protects someone's body in a fight. Knights often wore **armor**.

army

An **army** is a large group of people who fight together. —**armies**

around

Around means on all sides. Ben built a fence **around** his yard. Sandra looked **around** the room for her shoes.

armor

arrive

To **arrive** is to come to a place. Eric ran all the way to school so he would **arrive** on time. My cousin mailed me a letter, but it never **arrived.**

arrow

1. An **arrow** is a stick with a point at one end. You can shoot **arrows** from a bow. **2.** An **arrow** is a symbol. It is used to point in one direction.

arrow

art

art

Art is something made to be beautiful. Pictures, poems, and music are kinds of **art.**

artist

An **artist** is a person who makes art. You can see the work of many **artists** in a museum.

artist

as

As means the same amount. Dee and Kenny are the same height. Dee is **as** tall **as** Kenny.

ash

Ash is what is left after something burns. It is a soft gray powder. Ray watched his father clean the **ashes** out of the fireplace.

ashamed

Ashamed means feeling bad because of something you did. Sue felt **ashamed** because she lied to her sister.

ask

1. To **ask** means to say a question. The teacher **asks,** "Who knows the answer?"
2. To **ask** for something means to say that you want it. Oliver **asked** for more soup because he was hungry.

asleep

Asleep means sleeping. Anna was **asleep** until a loud noise woke her up.

asleep

astronaut

An **astronaut** is a person who goes into space. Some **astronauts** have walked on the moon.

at

1. At tells where a person or a thing is. Elena went to school this morning. She is **at** school now. **2. At** tells when something happens. School begins **at** nine o'clock. **3. At** also means toward. Jerry looked **at** the sky to watch for falling stars.

astronaut

ate

Ate is a form of **eat.** Chris eats three meals every day. Last night he **ate** pizza for supper.

attention

Attention is looking and listening with care. The crowd watched the magician do tricks with cards. They were interested in what he did. The magician had the crowd's **attention.**

attic

An **attic** is a room at the top of a house. An **attic** is a place to keep things you don't use every day.

attic

15

August

August is a month of the year. It has 31 days. **August** comes after July and before September.

aunt

An **aunt** is the sister of your mother or father. An **aunt** can also be the wife of your uncle. A person can have many **aunts** and uncles.

author

An **author** is someone who writes a story, a play, or a poem. Many **authors** write books for children.

automobile

automobile

Automobile is a another word for **car**. People drive **automobiles** on roads.

autumn

Autumn is a season. It comes after summer and before winter. School starts in **autumn**. Another word for **autumn** is **fall**.

awake

Awake means not asleep. David tried to stay **awake** all night.

away

1. Away shows distance. The ocean is three miles **away** from here. **2. Away** also shows direction. Danny walked **away** from the house and toward the street. **3.** To give something **away** means to give it to someone else. Dolly gave her bicycle to her cousin. She gave it **away** because she got a new one.

awful

Awful means very bad or terrible. When you have a cold you feel **awful.**

ax

An **ax** is a tool. It has a flat, sharp metal head and a long handle. **Axes** are used to cut wood.

awake

away

ax

A **B** C D E F G H I J K L M N O P Q R S T U V W X Y Z
a **b** c d e f g h i j k l m n o p q r s t u v w x y z

baby
A **baby** is a very young child. **Babies** eat and sleep a lot. —**babies**

back
1. The **back** is a part of the body. We like to lie on our **backs** and look up at the sky. **2. Back** is the opposite of front. The caboose is at the **back** of the train. **3.** To go **back** means to return. Students go **back** to school every fall.

baby

backward

1. Backward means in the opposite order. *Bat* spelled **backward** is *tab*. **2. Backward** also means toward the back. Jack looked **backward** to see if his brother was behind him.

backward

bad

1. Bad means not good. We couldn't eat the fruit because it was **bad. 2. Bad** also means not nice. Amy is angry. She is shouting at everybody. Amy is in a **bad** mood. **3. Bad** can mean able to hurt. Too much candy is **bad** for your teeth. **4. Bad** can also mean serious. Jody had a **bad** cold, so she stayed in bed.

bag

A **bag** is used to hold things. It can be made of paper, plastic, cloth, or leather. Jason brings his lunch to school in a paper **bag.**

bag

bake

To **bake** is to cook in the oven. John **baked** his pie for an hour.

ball

A **ball** is a round object. **Balls** of many sizes are used in games and sports.

ball

balloon

A **balloon** is a kind of bag filled with gas. Some **balloons** are huge and can carry people high into the sky.

balloon

banana

A **banana** is a kind of fruit. It has a long curved shape and a yellow skin.

band

band

A **band** is a group of people who play music together. Everyone in the parade marched to the music of the **band.**

bank

A **bank** is a safe place to keep money. A **bank** can be a small box or jar that you keep at home. A **bank** is also a big building. People can leave money or borrow it at the **bank.**

barber

A **barber** is a person who gives haircuts. **Barbers** work in **barber** shops.

bare

Bare means not covered with anything. Luis did not have any socks or shoes on. He was walking around with **bare** feet.

barber

bark

Bark is the skin of a tree. It is thick and rough. **Bark** covers the trunk and the branches.

barn

A **barn** is a kind of building on a farm. The **barn** is where the farm animals stay at night. Farm machines and food for the animals are kept in **barns,** too.

barn

barrel

A **barrel** is used to hold things. It is made of wood or metal. The top and the bottom of **barrels** are flat circles. Some **barrels** have curved sides.

barrel

base

1. A **base** is the bottom part of something. The statue in the park has a square **base**. The statue stands on its **base**. **2.** A **base** is a place where you are safe in a game. In baseball you try to run to all four **bases**.

baseball

baseball

1. Baseball is a sport. It is played by two teams with a bat and a ball. **2.** A **baseball** is the hard white ball used in a game of **baseball**.

basket

A **basket** is used to hold things. It can be made of strips of wood or grass. **Baskets** are often shaped like bowls and have handles.

basket

basketball

1. Basketball is a sport. It is played by two teams with a large ball and two baskets. **2.** A **basketball** is the large rubber ball used in a game of basketball.

bat[1]

A **bat** is a thick stick. It is used to hit a ball. **Bats** are made of wood, metal, or plastic.

basketball

bat²

bat²

A **bat** is a small animal. A **bat** has a body like a mouse and wings. **Bats** sleep during the day and fly around at night.

bath

A **bath** is washing the body with water. Jay takes a **bath** every night. He sits in water in the bathtub. He uses soap and a cloth to wash himself. Jay takes a **bath** to get clean.

bathroom

A **bathroom** is a room where you wash yourself. In Lee's house there are two **bathrooms.**

bathtub

A **bathtub** is used to hold water for a bath. You sit in the water to take a bath.

be

1. To **be** means to live or fill space. A person cannot **be** in two places at the same time. **2.** To **be** tells what something is like. Dogs can **be** big or small. Tomorrow will **be** sunny. —**is, was, been**

beach

beach

A **beach** is an area of sand at the edge of a lake or an ocean. **Beaches** are part of the shore.

beak

beak

A **beak** is part of a bird's mouth. It is hard and ends in a point. A bird's **beak** can be large or small.

bear

A **bear** is a large animal. It has thick fur and strong claws. Many **bears** sleep all winter.

bear

beat

1. To **beat** means to hit. Rich **beat** a drum when he marched in the parade. **2.** To **beat** eggs means to mix them up. You have to **beat** eggs to make a cake. **3.** To **beat** also means to win. Our team lost all its games this year. We could not **beat** anybody. —**beat, beaten**

beaten

Beaten is a form of **beat.** Fred's father asked Fred to beat the eggs, but Fred said he had **beaten** them already.

beautiful

Beautiful means very nice to look at. **Beautiful** can also mean very nice to listen to. Rainbows and music are **beautiful.**

beaver

beaver

A **beaver** is a kind of animal. It has a flat tail and large, strong front teeth. **Beavers** build dams across streams. They live in these dams.

became

Became is a form of **become.** Marcie wants to become a pilot one day. Her father **became** a pilot many years ago.

because

Because tells why something happens. Beth ate an apple **because** she was hungry. People read books **because** they want to learn.

become

To **become** means to change into something. A caterpillar changes into a moth. It **becomes** a moth inside a cocoon. The caterpillars **became** moths during the summer. —**became, become**

bed

bed

A **bed** is a kind of furniture. People sleep in **beds**.

bee

A **bee** is an insect. It can fly. Some **bees** make honey.

beef

Beef is a kind of meat. It comes from cattle. Hamburger is made from **beef**.

bee

been

Been is a form of **be**. Steve wants to be a farmer when he grows up. His parents have **been** farmers for many years.

before

1. **Before** means first. Minny washes her hands first and then she eats supper. Minny washes her hands **before** she eats. 2. **Before** also means in the past. Alice rode in a plane for the first time last week. She had never been on a plane **before**.

began

Began is a form of **begin**. The grass **began** to grow after it rained.

begin

To **begin** means to start. Grass **begins** to grow in the spring. It stops growing in the fall. —**began, begun**

begun

Begun is a form of **begin**. Dictionaries have always **begun** with the word *a*.

behave

To **behave** means to do things in some way. If Brad **behaves** well, his father will read him a story.

behind

Behind means at the back. Sally and Julio stood in line for juice. Sally stood in front of Julio. Julio stood **behind** Sally.

behind

believe

To **believe** means to think something is true. Anna **believes** everything her sister says.

bell

A **bell** is a hollow metal cup. Sometimes there is another piece of metal inside it. A **bell** rings when you hit it or shake it.

bell

belong

1. To **belong** means to feel good in a place. Fish **belong** in the water. **2.** To **belong** also means to be owned by somebody. That shirt **belongs** to Gordon. It is his shirt.

below

Below means under. Roots grow **below** the ground.

bend

To **bend** means to make a curve. Lee **bends** over to put water in her pail. —**bent**

bent

Bent is a form of **bend**. I **bent** my knees and jumped. Sara's glasses were **bent** after she sat on them.

bend

28

berry

A **berry** is a kind of fruit.
It is small and round.
Berries grow on bushes.
—**berries**

berry

beside

Beside means at the side
of. Kim and Don are sitting
together. Kim sits **beside**
Don and Don sits
beside Kim.

best

Best means better than
any other. Susan's **best**
friend is the friend she
likes most.

beside

better

Better means very good,
but not the best. Eddy
swims **better** than Mark.
Bill likes warm days **better**
than cold ones.

between

between

Between means in the middle. The letters *c a t* spell
cat. The *a* is **between** the *c* and the *t*.

beyond

Beyond means on the other side of something. Luana climbed over a fence and into the field. She went **beyond** the fence.

bicycle

A **bicycle** is a kind of machine. It has two big wheels, two handles, and a seat. You make a **bicycle** go by moving your legs.

bicycle

big

Big means not small. Whales and elephants are **big. Large** is another word for **big. —bigger, biggest**

bill

bill

A **bill** is a bird's beak. Ducks have big **bills.**

bird

A **bird** is a kind of animal. It has two wings and is covered with feathers. Robins, chickens, eagles, and ostriches are all **birds.** Most **birds** can fly.

bird

birth

Birth is the moment when a person is born. Most **births** happen in hospitals.

birthday

Your **birthday** is the day of your birth. Lynne was born on November 8. November 8 is her **birthday.**

bit

1. Bit is a form of **bite.** Ed **bit** into an apple. **2. Bit** also means a small amount. Ted put a **bit** of pepper into his soup.

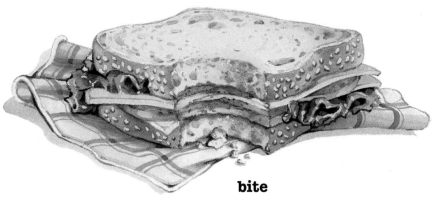

bite

bite

1. To **bite** means to cut with your teeth. Lisa is hungry. She **bites** her sandwich. Then she chews and swallows. **2.** A **bite** is a small amount you can cut off with your teeth. Lisa took a **bite** of her sandwich. She will eat the rest later. —**bit, bitten**

bitten

Bitten is a form of **bite.** My brother was **bitten** by a dog.

bitter

Bitter means having a sharp taste. Debbie tasted the medicine and made a face. It was very **bitter.**

black

Black is a color. **Black** is a very dark color. This sentence is printed in **black** ink.

blacksmith

blacksmith

A **blacksmith** is a person who makes things out of iron. **Blacksmiths** make horseshoes.

blanket

blanket

A **blanket** is a large soft cloth. People cover themselves with **blankets** to keep warm.

blew

Blew is a form of **blow**. Today it is calm, but yesterday the wind **blew** hard.

blind

Blind means not able to see. Anybody who cannot see is **blind.**

block

1. A **block** is a piece of wood or plastic or stone. It has straight sides and is usually shaped like a square or a rectangle. Children play with **blocks.** **2.** A **block** is an area of a city. It has four streets for sides. Tom and Jim walked around the **block.**

block

blood

Blood is a red liquid. **Blood** is inside our bodies. Nobody can live without **blood.**

blossom

A **blossom** is a flower. The **blossoms** on apple trees are white or pink.

blossom

blow

1. To **blow** means to push with air. The wind **blows** the leaves around on the ground. **2.** To **blow** means to make a sound by pushing air. We heard the whistle **blow.** It **blew** five times. —**blew, blown**

blown

Blown is a form of **blow.** The leaves were **blown** off the tree by the wind.

33

blue

Blue is a color. The sky is **blue** when no clouds cover it.

board

A **board** is a long, flat piece of wood. **Boards** are used to build houses.

board

boat

A **boat** carries people and things on the water. **Boats** can be made of wood, metal, or plastic. Most **boats** have engines to make them move. Some **boats** have sails.

boat

body

The **body** of a person is the part you can see and touch. Feet, hands, hearts, and brains are all parts of the **body.** All people and animals have **bodies. —bodies**

boil

To **boil** is to change from a liquid into a gas. When water **boils** it makes bubbles, and steam rises into the air.

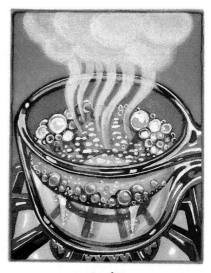

boil

bone

bone

A **bone** is a part of the body. It is hard. We cannot see our **bones,** but we can feel them under our skin.

book

A **book** is a group of pages. The pages have words and pictures on them. The pages are held together with thread or glue. This dictionary is a **book.**

book

boot

A **boot** is a large shoe. **Boots** are made of rubber or leather. Most people wear **boots** in the rain or snow.

border

A **border** is an edge. It is a line where one area ends and another begins. We made a **border** of stones around the garden.

boot

35

born

Born means brought into life. Terry is one day old. She was **born** yesterday.

borrow

To **borrow** means to get something that belongs to somebody else. You can use it for a small amount of time. Wally **borrowed** a book from the library. He has to return it in two weeks.

both

both

Both means two together. Naomi uses **both** hands to eat a sandwich.

bother

To **bother** means to give trouble. Jay's little sister **bothered** him with a lot of questions.

bottle

A **bottle** is used to hold liquids. It is made of glass or plastic. Al got a **bottle** of juice at the store.

bottle

bottom

The **bottom** is the lowest part of something. A tree has leaves at the top. It has roots at the **bottom.**

bought

Bought is a form of **buy.** Most people buy food at a store. Fran **bought** some this morning.

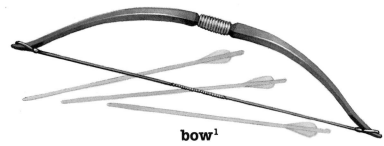

bow[1]

bow[1]

1. A **bow** is a curved piece of wood. A piece of string is tied to the ends of it. **Bows** are used to shoot arrows.
2. A **bow** is also a knot made with ribbon or string. It has two circles and two ends. I tie my shoes with a **bow.**

bow[2]

bow[2]

To **bow** means to bend the body forward. In the story the knight meets a king. He **bows** to the king with respect.

bowl

bowl

A **bowl** is used to hold things. **Bowls** are round and hollow. People eat soup and cereal out of them.

bowling

Bowling is a sport. **Bowling** is played with a heavy ball and pieces of wood shaped like bottles.

bowling

box

A **box** is used to hold things. It has four sides and a flat bottom. Some **boxes** have tops, too.

boy

A **boy** is a male child. **Boys** grow up to be men.

brain

The **brain** is a part of the body. It is inside your head. The **brain** makes our arms, legs, eyes, and ears work. People think with their **brains**.

box

branch

A **branch** is a part of a tree. **Branches** grow out from the trunk of a tree. Leaves grow from the **branches.**

brave

Brave means without fear. Ellen is afraid of dogs. She tries to be **brave** when she sees one in the park.

bread

Bread is a kind of food. It is made with flour and water and other things mixed together. **Bread** is baked in an oven.

break

1. To **break** means to divide into pieces. If a window **breaks,** it becomes pieces of glass. The window **broke** when a baseball went through it. **2.** To **break** also means not to work. If a machine **breaks,** someone has to fix it. Then it will work again. **3.** To **break** the law means to do something against the law. Someone who robs a bank is **breaking** the law. —**broke, broken**

branch

bread

break

breakfast

Breakfast is a meal. It is the first meal of the day. At **breakfast** Bud usually eats cereal with milk.

breakfast

breath

A **breath** is an amount of air. The air comes through our noses and into our bodies. The doctor asked Jenny to take a deep **breath**.

breathe

To **breathe** is to take in breaths of air. Jeff **breathes** fast when he runs.

bridge

bridge

A **bridge** is used to cross from one side to the other. **Bridges** are often built over water.

bright

Bright means giving a lot of light. The sun is very **bright**.

bring

To **bring** means to take something with you. When Carol goes to a birthday party, she **brings** a present.
—**brought**

broke

Broke is a form of **break.** It is easy for glass to break. Yesterday I dropped a glass. It **broke** into pieces.

broken

Broken is a form of **break.** That window has **broken** into five pieces of glass.

broom

A **broom** is a kind of tool. It is a long stick with straw tied to one end. Most people use **brooms** to clean dirt off floors.

broom

brother

A **brother** is a boy who has the same parents as somebody else. David and his **brother** Mike walk home from school together.

brought

Brought is a form of **bring.** Carol always brings presents to birthday parties. She **brought** one to Natasha's party last week.

brown

Brown is a color. Toast and chocolate are **brown.** Some people have **brown** hair.

brush

1. A **brush** is a kind of tool. It looks like a small broom. Some **brushes** are used to paint with. Other **brushes** are used to clean things.
2. To **brush** means to clean with a **brush**. Alan **brushes** his teeth every morning and night.

brush

bubble

A **bubble** is a round shape with air in it. **Bubbles** can be made in soap and water. **Bubbles** are also made when water boils.

bucket

A **bucket** is used to carry things. It can be made of wood, metal, or plastic. It has a flat round bottom and a handle. **Buckets** are often used to carry water.

bubble

build

To **build** means to put together. Alex used wood and nails to **build** a house for his dog. —**built**

building

A **building** is a place that has been built. Houses, hotels, schools, and barns are all **buildings**.

bucket

built

Built is a form of **build.** The carpenters **built** that house in one summer.

bull

bull

A **bull** is a large animal. It lives on a farm. **Bulls** have horns and eat grass.

bulldozer

bulldozer

A **bulldozer** is a very strong tractor. **Bulldozers** push dirt and rocks from one place to another.

bump

1. To **bump** means to hit against something. Duncan **bumped** his head on the table by accident. **2.** A **bump** is a round place that sticks out. The road had a lot of **bumps** in it.

burn

To **burn** is to be covered with fire. We like to watch the logs **burn** in the fireplace.

bus

bus

A **bus** is a machine. It has four wheels, an engine, and many seats and windows. **Buses** carry many people from one place to another.

bush

A **bush** is a plant. It has many branches and leaves. **Bushes** are not as big as trees. Some flowers grow on **bushes**.

bush

busy

Busy means doing many things. Abby has a lot of work to do. She is very **busy** today.

but

1. But is used to put two opposite ideas together. The weather was cold yesterday, **but** today it is warm. **2. But** means except. Tina, Ned, and Bob liked the new car. Albert did not like it. Everybody **but** Albert liked the new car.

butter

Butter is a kind of food. It is made from cow's milk. **Butter** is soft and yellow. Some people eat it on bread.

butterfly

A **butterfly** is an insect. It has four thin wings. These wings can have many colors. Some caterpillars change into **butterflies.**
—**butterflies**

butterfly

button

A **button** is a small round piece of wood or plastic. **Buttons** are sewn on clothes to keep them closed.

buy

To **buy** means to give money for something. You can **buy** all kinds of food at a supermarket.
—**bought**

button

by

1. **By** shows who or what does something. The question was asked **by** Dana. 2. **By** also shows how something is done. We made a garden **by** planting some flowers. 3. **By** can mean before some time. Nicole is usually hungry **by** supper.

45

A B C D E F G H I J K L M N O P Q R S T U V W X Y Z
a b c d e f g h i j k l m n o p q r s t u v w x y z

caboose

A **caboose** is the last car on a train. The people who work on the train eat and sleep in the **caboose**.

cage

A **cage** is a kind of box. The sides are made of metal or wood poles. Birds and other animals are sometimes kept in **cages**.

caboose

cake

A **cake** is a kind of food. It is made of flour, sugar, eggs, and milk. It is baked in an oven. **Cakes** are sweet.

call

1. To **call** means to say in a loud voice. I heard the teacher **call** my name. **2.** To **call** means to use the telephone. Chuck **calls** his friends on the telephone almost every day. **3.** To **call** means to give a name to. Anne **calls** her doll Emily. **4.** A **call** is a loud sound made by a person. The police heard someone's **call** for help.

calm

1. Calm means quiet and not moving. The wind is **calm** today. **2. Calm** means quiet and not bothered. Tim is very **calm** about his first day at school.

came

Came is a form of **come**. Bill **came** into the kitchen. He comes into the kitchen to eat supper.

camel

camel

A **camel** is a large animal. It has long legs and a long neck. It also has one or two humps on its back. **Camels** can carry people and things across the desert.

camera

A **camera** is a small machine that makes pictures. People often take **cameras** along on their vacations.

camera

camp

1. A **camp** is a place where people live outside. They sleep in tents or huts and cook over a fire. Many children go to a **camp** in the summer. **2.** To **camp** means to live in a camp. Sally and her family **camped** near the lake.

can¹

Can means to be able to. Kelly **can** run fast. Sal **can** speak two languages. **—could**

can²

can²

A **can** is used to hold things. It is usually made of metal and comes all in one piece. You can buy paint in **cans.**

candle

A **candle** is a stick of wax with a piece of string in it. **Candles** make light when they burn.

candle

candy

Candy is a kind of food. It is made of sugar and is very sweet. **Candy** can be made with chocolate, nuts, or fruit. —**candies**

cannot

Cannot means is not able to. A dog can run, but it **cannot** fly.

canoe

canoe

A **canoe** is a kind of small boat. It is long, narrow, and light. **Canoes** go through the water very quietly.

can't

Can't is a short way to say **cannot**. Fish can swim, but they **can't** talk.

cap

A **cap** is a kind of hat. People who play baseball wear **caps.**

cap

car

1. A **car** is a machine. It has four wheels, an engine, seats, and windows. People travel over roads in **cars.**
2. A **car** is also one part of a train. It is like a big room on wheels. Most trains have several **cars.**

car

card

1. A **card** is a small piece of thick paper. It is shaped like a rectangle. **Cards** have numbers and pictures on them. People play games with **cards.**
2. A **card** is also a small folded piece of paper. It has a message on it. You send **cards** to people in the mail.

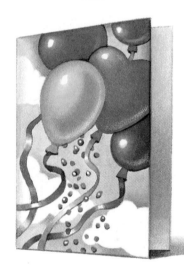

card

care

1. Care means a slow, steady way of doing things so that nothing bad will happen. You have to handle knives and other tools with **care. 2. Care** also means keeping someone or something safe. Children are in the **care** of their parents. **3.** To **care** means to have a special interest in something. Nancy **cares** about her pets.

careful

To be **careful** means to use care. Juanita is **careful** when she crosses the street. She watches for cars and thinks about what she is doing.

carpenter

A **carpenter** is a person who builds things with wood. **Carpenters** also fix the wood parts of houses and ships.

carrot

carrot

A **carrot** is a kind of vegetable. It is long and orange. **Carrots** grow under the ground.

carry

To **carry** means to hold something and take it somewhere. Lindsay **carries** her lunch in a bag.
—**carries, carried**

carry

cartoon

A **cartoon** is a kind of picture. It is drawn by an artist in a simple way. **Cartoons** are usually funny.

castle

A **castle** is a large building with high thick walls. **Castles** were built a long time ago. Kings, queens, and knights lived in **castles**.

castle

cat

A **cat** is a small animal. It has four legs, soft fur, and a long tail. Many people have **cats** as pets.

cat

catch

To **catch** means to take and hold something that is moving. Greg throws the ball for Mindy to **catch**. He threw the ball and she **caught** it.
—**caught**

caterpillar

A **caterpillar** is an insect. It looks like a worm covered with fur. **Caterpillars** change into butterflies or moths.

caterpillar

cattle

Cattle are large animals. They have four legs and two horns. They are raised for milk and meat. Cows and bulls are **cattle**.

caught

Caught is a form of **catch**. Lee threw the ball, and Donna **caught** it.

cattle

cause

1. To **cause** is to make something happen. Sometimes Will and Ellie **cause** a lot of noise. **2.** A **cause** is the person or thing that makes something happen. The storm was the **cause** of the flood.

cave

cave

A **cave** is a hollow place that goes deep under the ground. **Caves** are very dark inside.

ceiling

A **ceiling** is the top side of a room. You walk on the floor. You look up at the **ceiling.**

cellar

A **cellar** is a room under a house.

cent

A **cent** is an amount of money. A nickel is five **cents,** and a dollar is 100 **cents.**

center

The **center** is the middle of something. Kim's doughnut had jelly in the **center.**

cereal

Cereal is a kind of food. Many **cereals** are made from corn, wheat, or rice. Most people eat **cereal** with milk in a bowl.

cereal

chair

A **chair** is a kind of furniture. It has four legs and a seat. People sit on **chairs**.

chance

1. Chance means luck. I found three dollars by **chance**. **2. Chance** means that something may happen. There is a **chance** it will rain today. **Chances** are it will rain all day.

chair

change

1. To **change** means to become different. In the fall, leaves **change** color from green to red, orange, and yellow. **2.** To **change** means to put on other clothes. After school Arthur and Pablo **change** before they go out to play. **3. Change** means coins. Joyce has a dollar and some **change**.

chase

1. To **chase** means to run after something to try to catch it. We **chased** our dog around the yard. **2.** A **chase** is when someone follows something quickly. Many car **chases** end in accidents.

check

1. A **check** is a mark. You make a **check** next to something to show that it is right. A **check** looks like this: . **2.** To **check** also means to look for something. Mary can't find her shoes. Her mother tells her to **check** under her bed. **3.** A **check** is also a square. Lucy's shirt has big red and white **checks** all over it.

check

cheek

A **cheek** is a part of the body. Your face has two **cheeks.** They are the wide soft areas below your eyes.

cheerful

To be **cheerful** means to act happy. Our new neighbor smiles a lot. He says nice things to everybody. He is always **cheerful.**

cheek

cheese

Cheese is a kind of food. It is made from milk. **Cheese** can be hard or soft. Many **cheeses** are yellow or white.

cherry

A **cherry** is a kind of fruit. It is small, round, and red. **Cherries** grow on **cherry** trees.

cherry

chest

1. The **chest** is a part of the body. It is between your neck and your stomach. **2.** A **chest** is a strong box. Many **chests** have locks.

chest

chew

To **chew** means to break something into small pieces with the teeth. Our puppy **chewed** an old shoe.

chicken

1. A **chicken** is a kind of bird. **Chickens** are raised for eggs and meat. **2.** Chicken is a kind of meat. It comes from a chicken.

chicken

chief

A **chief** is a person who leads other people. **Chiefs** decide how a group of people will do their jobs. Firefighters and the police have **chiefs.**

child

A **child** is a very young person. Boys and girls are **children. —children**

children

Children means more than one **child. Children** grow up to be men and women.

chimney

A **chimney** is a long hollow part above a fireplace. Smoke and gas from the fireplace go up the **chimney** to the outside.

chin

A **chin** is a part of the body. It is at the bottom of your face, below your mouth.

chimney

chocolate

Chocolate is a kind of food. It is usually brown and very sweet. Candy and cake are often made with **chocolate**.

choose

To **choose** means to take one thing from a lot of things. There are many books to **choose** from at the library. Abby **chose** a book about horses.
—**chose, chosen**

chose

Chose is a form of **choose**. Marie and Etta **chose** to play soccer. Sometimes they choose to play cards or marbles.

chosen

Chosen is a form of **choose**. Anne must choose a kind of sandwich for lunch. She has **chosen** a peanut butter sandwich.

57

Christmas

Christmas is a holiday.
It comes each year
on December 25.

circle

A **circle** is a round shape.
It is made by a line that
turns until the two ends
touch. **Circles** do not have
any corners or straight parts.

circle

circus

circus

A **circus** is a kind of show. **Circuses** usually happen
in a big tent. You can see clowns, magicians, and
animals at the **circus**.

city

A **city** is a place where many people live and work. It
has many streets and tall buildings. There are a lot of
cities in our country. —**cities**

class

A **class** is a group of students who learn together.
Our **class** went on a trip to the museum.

claw

A **claw** is a part of the foot of an animal or a bird. It is sharp and curved. Birds hold on to branches with their **claws.**

clay

Clay is a kind of earth. Pots and cups can be made from **clay.**

claw

clean

1. Clean means without any dirt. Blake keeps his dog **clean.** He gives him a bath every Saturday. **2.** To **clean** is to take away dirt. Dolly **cleaned** her face with soap and water.

clear

Clear means easy to see through. The water in the lake was so **clear** we could see the bottom.

clever

Clever means able to think quickly. Jaime always invents good stories. He is very **clever** with words.

climb

To **climb** means to use your hands and feet to move up or down. I like to **climb** trees. We **climbed** a mountain on our vacation.

climb

clock

A **clock** is a kind of machine. It tells what time it is.

close

1. **Close** means near. Some flowers grew **close** to that wall. 2. To **close** something means to keep the inside in and the outside out. Laura **closed** the door after she came into the room. 3. To **close** is to become shut. The store **closes** at the same time every night.

closet

A **closet** is a very small room. People keep clothes, shoes, and other things in **closets**.

cloth

Cloth is used to make clothes. It comes from cotton, wool, and other things.

clothes

Clothes cover a person's body. Coats, shirts, dresses, pants, and socks are all kinds of **clothes**.

cloud

A **cloud** is a white or gray shape in the sky. **Clouds** are made of drops of water.

clock

clothes

clown

A **clown** is a person who makes people laugh. **Clowns** wear funny costumes. They play tricks. Many **clowns** work in a circus.

coat

A **coat** is something that covers your body. **Coats** are usually made from thick cloth. They keep you warm when the weather is cold.

cocoon

A **cocoon** is a ball of threads made by some caterpillars. These caterpillars live in **cocoons** before they change into moths.

clown

coin

A **coin** is a kind of money. **Coins** are usually round. They are made of metal. Pennies, nickels, dimes, and quarters are all **coins.**

cold

1. To be **cold** means to have a low temperature. Snow and ice are **cold. 2.** When you have a **cold** you are sick. Your head may hurt. You may sneeze a lot. People with **colds** often rest in bed.

collect

To **collect** means to put things together in a group. We **collected** our toys into a pile.

color

Color is the kind of light that comes from a thing. Most things have a **color**. Red, yellow, green, and blue are **colors**.

color

come

To **come** is to move toward. Billy's mother asked him to **come** to the table to eat supper. He **came** quickly because he was hungry. —**came, come**

complete

Complete means with all the parts together. We worked on the puzzle until it was **complete**.

computer

A **computer** is a machine. It works with numbers, words, pictures, and sound. **Computers** can work very quickly.

computer

cone

1. A **cone** is an object with a circle at one end and a point at the other. Many people eat ice cream in **cones**. 2. A **cone** is a part of some kinds of trees. A pine **cone** has the seeds for new pine trees inside it.

cone

confuse

1. To **confuse** means to mix things up in your mind. I can't understand my sister. She **confuses** me when she talks. **2.** To **confuse** also means to think one thing is another. My teachers sometimes **confuse** me with my brother.

consonant

A **consonant** is a kind of letter. B, C, D, F, G, H, J, K, L, M, N, P, Q, R, S, T, V, W, X, and Z are **consonants. Consonants** and vowels make the letters of the alphabet.

contest

A **contest** is a kind of game to see who can win. Two or more people can be in a **contest.**

continue

To **continue** means to start again. We played baseball all morning. Then we **continued** the game after lunch.

control

To **control** something means to make it do what you want it to do. David **controls** his kite with a long string.
—**controlled**

cook

1. To **cook** is to heat food to make it ready to eat. We **cooked** the turkey in the oven for six hours. **2.** A **cook** is a person who makes meals. **Cooks** work in kitchens.

cook

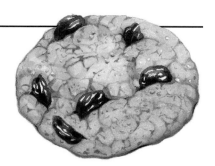
cookie

cookie

A **cookie** is a kind of food. It is like a small flat cake. **Cookies** are sweet.

cool

Cool means not very cold. The weather was **cool** this morning, but it got warm this afternoon.

copper

Copper is a kind of metal. Pennies and wire are made from **copper**.

copy

copy

1. To **copy** something is to make another one like it. Abel prints a poem on a piece of paper. He **copied** the poem out of a book. 2. A **copy** is something made to look like something else. Laura drew a picture. Then she made a **copy** of it to give to her friend.

corn

Corn is a kind of vegetable. It grows on a tall green plant. **Corn** can be yellow or white.

corn

corner

A **corner** is the place where two sides come together. Squares and rectangles have four **corners.**

correct

1. **Correct** means without mistakes. Jack's answer was **correct. 2.** To **correct** means to check for mistakes in something. The teacher **corrects** all our tests.

cost

To **cost** means to have a price of some amount of money. The book Susan wants **costs** a dollar, but she only has 50 cents. —**cost**

costume

A **costume** is a set of special clothes. Stacy wore a **costume** in the school play.

cotton

Cotton is soft, light, and gray. It grows on a **cotton** plant. It is made into cloth. People wear clothes made from **cotton** in the summer.

costume

could

Could is a form of **can.** Tom can whistle. He **could** whistle when he was five years old.

couldn't

Couldn't is a short way to say **could not.** Last year A.J. **couldn't** read as well as Tyrone, but now he can.

count

To **count** means to add. Kate **counted** the pencils on her desk. There were five pencils.

country

1. A **country** is a place where people live. All the people in one **country** share the same laws. There are many cities and towns in a **country**. There are many **countries** in the world. 2. The **country** is an area away from a city. There are forests, fields, and farms in the **country**. —**countries**

cousin

Your **cousin** is the child of your aunt or uncle. Ted has lots of **cousins**.

cover

1. To **cover** means to put something on top of something else. Wendy **covered** herself with thick blankets to keep warm.
2. A **cover** goes on the top or outside of something. Books have **covers**. Pots and pans also have **covers**.

cover

cow

A **cow** is a large animal that lives on a farm. **Cows** give milk.

cowboy

A **cowboy** is a man who takes care of cattle. **Cowboys** work on big farms. They often ride horses.

cow

cowgirl

A **cowgirl** is a woman who takes care of cattle. **Cowgirls** work on big farms. They often ride horses.

crack

A **crack** is a small broken place. It looks like a crooked line. The mirror had **cracks** in it.

cowboy/cowgirl

crash

1. To **crash** means to hit something and break with a lot of noise. We saw two cars **crash** into each other.
2. A **crash** is a loud noise. We heard a **crash** in the next room.

crack

crawl

To **crawl** is to move on your hands and knees. Babies **crawl** until they learn to walk.

crayon

A **crayon** is a piece of colored wax. It is used to draw and write with. **Crayons** come in many colors.

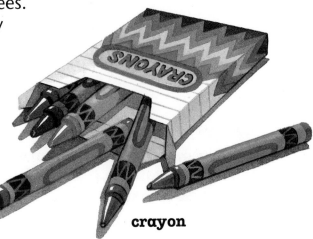

crayon

crocodile

cream

Cream is a kind of food. It is part of the milk that comes from a cow. Butter is made from **cream.**

crocodile

A **crocodile** is a very large reptile. It looks like an alligator with a long narrow jaw. **Crocodiles** live in rivers and swamps.

crooked

Crooked means not straight. Lightning looks like a **crooked** line in the sky.

crooked

cross

1. A **cross** is a shape. It is made by two lines that touch in the middle. It looks like this: + .
2. To **cross** means to go to the other side. The bridge **crosses** the river.

crow

A **crow** is a large bird with black feathers. **Crows** can make a loud noise.

crow

crowd

crowd

A **crowd** is a large group of people. **Crowds** come to watch football games.

cry

To **cry** is to have tears fall from your eyes. People sometimes **cry** when they are sad. —**cries, cried**

cup

A **cup** is used to hold liquid. It has a handle on the side. **Cups** are usually round. You can drink milk, water, or juice from a **cup.**

curious

To be **curious** is to want to learn. Karen asks a lot of questions. She is very **curious.**

cup

curly

Curly means twisting around in small circles. Leigh's hair is **curly,** but Kerry's is straight.

curve

1. A **curve** is a round line. The bottom of a U is a **curve.**
2. To **curve** means to follow a round line. This road **curves** to the left.

curly

cut

cut

To **cut** is to divide something into pieces with a sharp tool. Dan used scissors to **cut** pictures out of the newspaper.

A B C D E F G H I J K L M N O P Q R S T U V W X Y Z

a b c d e f g h i j k l m n o p q r s t u v w x y z

daisy

A **daisy** is a kind of
flower. Most **daisies**
are white with yellow
centers. —**daisies**

dam

A **dam** is a wall
across a river.
It causes a lake
to form behind it.
The **dam** controls
how water goes
from the lake
to the other side.

dam

damp

Damp means not very wet. Eric used a **damp** cloth to wash the table.

dance

To **dance** means to move your body to music. Marta **danced** with her friends at the party.

dandelion

A **dandelion** is a kind of flower. **Dandelions** are round and yellow.

dandelion

danger

Danger is something that can hurt you. Tornadoes can put people in **danger**.

dark

Dark means without light. At night it is **dark** outside.

date

A **date** is any one day. July 7 is a **date**. November 20 is also a **date**. Every day has a **date**.

daughter

A **daughter** is a person's female child. Bonnie's parents have two **daughters**. One is Bonnie and the other is Sue.

day

1. A **day** is the time from one morning to the next morning. There are 24 hours in one **day**. There are seven **days** in one week. 2. **Day** is the time when it is light outside. Rolf played outside all **day**. He only went in the house when it got dark.

dead

Dead means not alive. Plants and flowers die without water. They become **dead.**

dear

Something **dear** is something you love. People also use **dear** to begin a letter. Susan's letter to her aunt began with "**Dear** Aunt Kate."

December

December is the last month of the year. It has 31 days. **December** comes after November and before January.

decide

To **decide** means to choose. Ramona **decided** to wear a red shirt and blue pants.

deer

deep

Deep means going very far down. The ocean is **deep.**

deer

A **deer** is an animal. It has four legs and soft brown fur. **Deer** live in forests and fields. —**deer**

delicious

Delicious means very good to taste. We enjoyed a **delicious** lunch.

dentist

A **dentist** is a doctor who takes care of people's teeth.

describe

To **describe** means to tell or write all about something. I **described** my summer vacation to my friends.

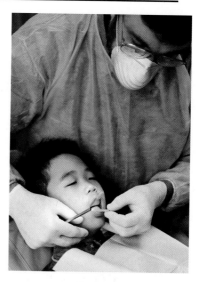

dentist

desert

A **desert** is a large dry area of land. Not much rain falls there. **Deserts** are covered by sand.

desert

design

A **design** is a group of different shapes and colors that is drawn or painted. The cards had pretty **designs** on one side.

desk

A **desk** is a kind of furniture. It has a large flat top and legs. People sit at **desks** to read and write.

desk

dessert

A **dessert** is a kind of food. It is the last part of a meal. **Dessert** is usually sweet. Ice cream, pie, cake, and fruit are **desserts**.

dessert

diamond

1. A **diamond** is a jewel. **Diamonds** are clear and very hard. **2.** A **diamond** is also a shape. It has four sides and four corners. One corner is at the top and another is at the bottom.

diamond

dictionary

A **dictionary** is a kind of book. It shows how words are spelled. It also explains what words mean. This book is a **dictionary**.
— **dictionaries**

did

Did is a form of **do.** Bob and Joe **did** something together. They went to the movies.

didn't

Didn't is a short way to say **did not.** Rick was sick. He **didn't** feel well at all. He **didn't** go to school.

die

To **die** means to become dead. The cold weather made all the flowers **die.** The leaves on the trees **died** too.

75

different

Different means not alike. Birds and fish are very **different** kinds of animals. A dog's tail is **different** from a cat's tail.

dig

To **dig** means to make a hole in the earth. Henrietta likes to **dig** in the garden. —**dug**

dig

dime

A **dime** is a coin. One **dime** is the same as ten pennies or two nickels. A dollar is ten **dimes**.

dinner

dinner

Dinner is a meal. It is the big meal of the day. Some people eat **dinner** at noon. Some people eat **dinner** at night.

dinosaur

dinosaur

A **dinosaur** is a reptile. It lived a long time ago. Some **dinosaurs** were huge and some were very small. Some **dinosaurs** ate plants and some ate meat.

dip

To **dip** means to put something in liquid and then take it out quickly. Dawn **dips** her cookies in milk before she eats them. —**dipped**

direction

1. A **direction** is somewhere you can look or point or go. North, south, east, and west are **directions**. 2. **Directions** tell you how to get somewhere. Matt and Arnie gave us the **directions** to their house. 3. **Directions** can also tell you how to do something. Games usually come with **directions**.

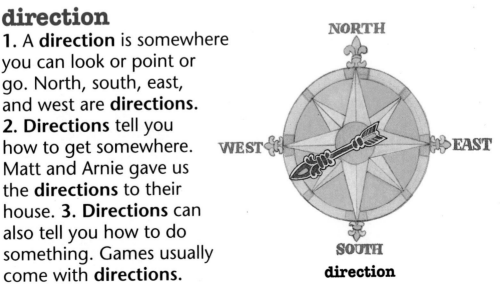

direction

dirt

Dirt means earth. The ground is made of **dirt** and rocks. Luke gets **dirt** on his clothes when he plays outside.

dirty

Dirty means covered with dirt. Our dog gets **dirty** when he swims in the swamp.

disappear

To **disappear** means to stop being seen. The sun **disappeared** behind a cloud.

dish

A **dish** is something to put food in. **Dishes** are usually round. Mike washed all the **dishes** after supper.

dish

distance

Distance is the space between two things. Airplanes can travel long **distances** in a few hours.

dive

To **dive** means to jump in. Elsa learned how to **dive** and swim at the lake.

dive

divide

To **divide** means to change one big thing into two or more smaller things. Mary **divided** the apple into two halves. Joel **divides** his toys in three piles.

do

To **do** means to make something happen. Hannah always **does** a good job cleaning her room. She has always **done** it without being asked. Hannah and Laura **did** some work together.
—**does, did, done**

dock

dock

A **dock** is a place to tie up a boat. Tim ties a rope to his boat when it is at the **dock.**

doctor

doctor

A **doctor** is a person who helps sick people get well. Many **doctors** work in hospitals.

does

Does is a form of **do**. Ben **does** his homework every night. Sue **does** hers, too.

doesn't

Doesn't is a short way to say **does not**. Larry **doesn't** like to eat carrots, but he does like corn.

dog

dog

A **dog** is an animal. It has four legs, fur, and a tail. Many people have **dogs** as pets. There are many kinds of **dogs**.

doll

A **doll** is a kind of toy. It looks like a baby or a small child.

doll

dollar

dollar

A **dollar** is an amount of money. A **dollar** is usually made of a piece of green paper shaped like a rectangle. One **dollar** is the same as 100 pennies.

done

Done is a form of **do.** Al fed his pets. He has **done** his job for the day.

donkey

A **donkey** is an animal. It looks like a small horse with long ears. **Donkeys** can carry heavy loads.

donkey

don't

Don't is a short way to say **do not.** Fish live in water. They **don't** live in trees.

door

A **door** is a place in a wall where you can walk through. You can usually open a **door** to go through. Then you close the **door** behind you.

dot

A **dot** is a small round spot. The letter *i* has a **dot** over it.

doughnut

A **doughnut** is a small round cake. Many **doughnuts** have a hole in the center. Some have jelly in the center. People like to eat **doughnuts** for breakfast.

doughnut

down

1. Down means going from a high place to a low place. A big balloon came **down** in our garden.
2. Down means in a low place. There is water **down** in the well.

Dr.

Dr. is a short way to write **doctor.** People use **Dr.** with a doctor's name. Our family doctor is **Dr.** Smith.

dragon

A **dragon** is a monster in stories. It is not real. **Dragons** look like huge reptiles with wings and claws. They breathe fire.

dragon

drank

Drank is a form of **drink.** Sam **drank** his milk quickly. He does not usually drink so fast.

draw

To **draw** is to make a picture. You can **draw** with pencils, pens, or crayons. Abel likes to **draw.**
—drew, drawn

draw

drawn

Drawn is a form of **draw.** Carol has **drawn** a picture of Nick. Now Nick will draw one of Carol.

dream

1. A **dream** is pictures or stories that happen in your mind when you sleep. **2.** To **dream** means to imagine stories while you sleep. One night Tina **dreamed** she could fly.

dress

1. To **dress** means to put clothes on. Jay's father helped him **dress** for the party. **2.** A **dress** is a kind of clothes. It is one piece that covers the top and the bottom of the body. Women and girls wear **dresses**.

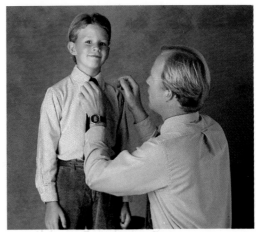

dress

drew

Drew is a form of **draw**. Andy used a red crayon to draw a circle on the paper. Then he **drew** some squares with a blue crayon.

drink

1. A **drink** is a liquid you can swallow. Orange juice is Tom's favorite **drink**. **2.** To **drink** means to take liquid into your mouth and swallow it. Bruce always **drinks** milk with supper. —**drank, drunk**

drive

To **drive** is to make a car, a truck, or a train go. My sister is old enough to **drive** a car. Yesterday she **drove** us to the beach. —**drove, driven**

driven

Driven is a form of **drive**. Engineers drive trains. Tim's uncle is an engineer. He has **driven** trains for most of his life.

drop

1. A **drop** is a very small amount of liquid. I felt a **drop** of rain on my nose. **2.** To **drop** something means to let it fall. Peter **dropped** his books and papers. Everybody **drops** things by accident sometimes. —**dropped**

drop

drove

Drove is a form of **drive**. When Carla missed the bus, her father **drove** her to school.

drugstore

A **drugstore** is a store where people can buy medicine. **Drugstores** also sell newspapers and other things.

drum

A **drum** is an instrument. It is round. To play a **drum** you beat on it with your hands or sticks.

drunk

Drunk is a form of **drink**. Terry drinks a lot of water. She has **drunk** nearly a whole bottle today.

drum

dry

1. Dry means not wet. During the storm we stayed warm and **dry** inside. **2.** To **dry** means to take all the water from something. The clothes hang outside to **dry**. The sun **dries** them in a few hours.
—**dries, dried**

dry

duck

A **duck** is a kind of bird. It has a wide flat bill and short legs. **Ducks** swim on rivers and lakes.

dug

Dug is a form of **dig**. Jason digs in the sand at the beach. He **dug** a big hole with his pail and shovel.

duck

dull

1. Dull means not sharp. It is hard to cut anything with **dull** scissors. **2. Dull** means not interesting. Tony didn't like the story. He thought it was **dull.**

during

During means the whole time. It is light outside **during** the day. We stayed inside **during** the storm.

dust

Dust is tiny pieces of dirt. **Dust** can make you sneeze. Wind blows **dust** around on dirt roads.

85

A B C D **E** F G H I J K L M N O P Q R S T U V W X Y Z

a b c d **e** f g h i j k l m n o p q r s t u v w x y z

each

Each means with none left out. Nan picked berries off a bush. She put **each** berry carefully in her basket.

each other

Each other means one and the other. Karen and Joy like **each other.** Russ and Larry saw **each other** at the fair.

eagle

An **eagle** is a kind of large bird. It has a curved beak and strong wings. Some **eagles** hunt small animals.

eagle

86

ear

An **ear** is a part of the body. There is one **ear** on each side of your head. People hear with their two **ears**.

early

1. Early means after a short time. Bobby gets up **early** in the morning.
2. Early also means before the usual time. Last night my brother and I went to bed **early**.

earn

To **earn** is to get something for what you do. Carly **earns** money sometimes by working in her neighbors' yards.

earth

1. Earth means dirt. There is good **earth** in the garden for the plants to grow in.
2. The **earth** is our world. The **earth** is covered by land and oceans.

ear

earn

earth

earthquake

An **earthquake** happens when a part of the earth moves suddenly. The ground shakes and sometimes buildings fall down during an **earthquake**.

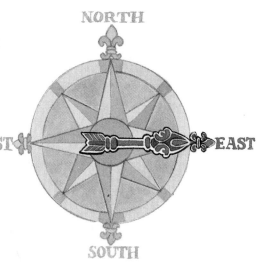

east

east

East is a direction. The sun rises in the **east**. **East** is the opposite of west.

easy

Easy means not hard to do. Fran thinks it is **easy** to ride a bicycle.

eat

eat

To **eat** means to take food into the body through the mouth. People **eat** when they feel hungry. I **ate** some soup for lunch. —**ate, eaten**

echo

An **echo** is a sound that comes back again. If you shout at a mountain, you may hear **echoes** of your voice.

edge

An **edge** is the line or place where something ends. The children played at the **edge** of the pond. The **edge** of a knife is very sharp.

edge

egg

An **egg** is a smooth round shell with a baby animal inside of it. Birds grow inside **eggs** until they are ready to hatch. Many people eat **eggs** from chickens for breakfast.

eight

Eight is a number. **Eight** is one more than seven. **Eight** is written **8.** 7 + 1 = **8.**

egg

either

1. **Either** means one or the other. For her birthday Becky wants **either** a puppy or a pony. She would be happy to get **either** of them.
2. **Either** means not also. Jeff did not want to play soccer. He did not want to play basketball **either.**

elbow

An **elbow** is a part of the body. Your arm bends at the **elbow.** Ellen sat with her **elbows** on the table.

elbow

electricity

Electricity is a kind of energy. It makes lamps light up. **Electricity** also makes refrigerators, computers, and many other things work.

elephant

An **elephant** is a very large animal. It has thick skin, big ears, and a long trunk. **Elephants** are the biggest animals that live on land.

elephant

else

Else means other or different. Molly did not want a turkey sandwich for lunch. She wanted something **else.**

emerald

An **emerald** is a kind of jewel. **Emeralds** are green.

emerald

empty

Empty means with nothing inside. Ray drank all his juice. He left his **empty** glass on the table.

empty

end

1. An **end** is the last part of something. This train has a caboose at the **end. 2.** An **end** is also either side of something long. My brother sat at one **end** of the table and I sat at the other. **3.** To **end** means to come to the last part. The story **ends** with a surprise.

energy

Energy is what makes things happen. Heat, light, and electricity are forms of **energy.** —**energies**

engine

An **engine** is a kind of machine. It burns oil, gas, or wood to do work. Cars, ships, and planes have **engines** to make them move.

engineer

engineer

1. An **engineer** is a person who drives a train. **Engineers** work the engines in the front of trains.
2. An **engineer** is also someone who tells people how to make engines, machines, or buildings.

enjoy

To **enjoy** something means to like it. We all **enjoyed** our vacation this year. We especially **enjoy** vacations in the country.

enough

Enough means as much or as many as you need. We have **enough** food for everybody.

enter

enter

To **enter** means to go into a place. Tara and P.J. **entered** the building together.

equal

equal

Equal means the same in amount or size. One dime is **equal** to ten pennies.

especially

Especially means more than anything else. Joelle likes to do a lot of things. She **especially** likes to act in plays.

even

1. **Even** means all at the same height. Todd made his bed so that the blanket was smooth and **even**.
2. An **even** number is a number that you can get to when you count by twos. Two, four, six, eight, and ten are **even** numbers.

evening

evening
Evening is the part of the day after the sun goes down. An **evening** ends when you go to bed. We stay at home most **evenings**.

ever
Ever means at any time. Have you **ever** seen an elephant?

every
Every means each one. Nobody could read **every** book in the library.

everybody
Everybody means every person. **Everybody** in my family likes to fish.

everyone
Everyone means everybody. **Everyone** at the party had a good time.

everything
Everything means every thing. After the storm the snow covered **everything**.

everywhere

Everywhere means in every place. Dana looked **everywhere** for his cat. Then he found her in the closet.

evil

To be **evil** is to try to hurt people. In the story an **evil** wizard used magic to turn the prince and princess into donkeys.

excellent

Excellent means very, very good. T.J. makes **excellent** cookies. Betty had an **excellent** idea.

except

Except means leaving out. Everyone **except** Jane was in class today. She was the only one who did not come to the class.

exciting

exciting

To be **exciting** is to make people feel a lot of energy. We read an **exciting** story. Tim felt a little afraid of the fireworks, but he thought they were **exciting,** too.

excuse

An **excuse** explains the reason for something. Students must bring a written **excuse** from their parents if they are late for school.

exercise

1. Exercise is running and jumping and moving your body around. Grace and Jeannie get a lot of **exercise** when they play in the park. **2.** An **exercise** lets you practice how to do something. We are learning to add by doing the **exercises** in our book.

exercise

exit

An **exit** is the way out of a room or a building. Our classroom has two **exits**.

expand

To **expand** is to get bigger. A balloon **expands** when you blow air into it.

expand

expect

To **expect** is to think something will happen. Kathy **expects** her father to be home in a few minutes.

expensive

Expensive means costing a lot of money. Robert's parents wanted to buy a new car, but cars were too **expensive**.

explain

To **explain** means to tell about something so that other people can understand it. Paul **explained** the rules of the game so we could all play it.

explore

explore

To **explore** means to go into a place you have never been before to see what is there. Some people like to **explore** caves and jungles. People also **explore** underwater and other places.

extra

Extra means more than what you need or expect. Mr. Green gave Toni five dollars to clean his car. She got an **extra** dollar for washing the tires.

eye

An **eye** is a part of the body. People and animals see with their two **eyes.** Your **eyes** are in the middle of your face.

eye

A B C D E F G H I J K L M N O P Q R S T U V W X Y Z

a b c d e f g h i j k l m n o p q r s t u v w x y z

face

1. The **face** is the front of the head. The eyes, the nose, and the mouth are all part of the **face. 2.** The **face** of a clock shows what time it is. Clock **faces** have numbers on them. **3.** To **face** means to look in some direction. Eric **faced** the front of the room.

fact

A **fact** is something that is true. Scientists try to find out the **facts.**

face

fair¹

To be **fair** means to treat everyone the same. Breaking the rules is not **fair.**

fair²

fair²

A **fair** is a place where people go to have fun. Some people show things there that they have grown or made. At most **fairs** there are machines to ride on and games to play.

fairy

A **fairy** is a small person in a story. **Fairy** stories are about magic. —**fairies**

fall

1. To **fall** is to go down. Anna still **falls** sometimes when she skates. 2. To **fall** asleep means to go to sleep. Paul **fell** asleep early last night. 3. **Fall** is a season. It comes after summer and before winter. **Fall** is another name for autumn. —**fell, fallen**

fall

fallen

Fallen is a form of **fall**.
All the leaves have **fallen**
off the trees by November.

family

A **family** is a group of
people who live together.
Families often have
a father, a mother, and
their children.
—**families**

fancy

fancy

Fancy means prettier or
better than usual. Janet
wore a **fancy** new dress
to the party.

far

Far means at a distance.
The moon is **far** away
from here. It takes
a long time to get there.

far

farm

A **farm** is an area of land.
People grow food and
raise animals on **farms**.

farmer

A **farmer** is someone
who works on a farm.
Farmers start to work
early in the morning.

farm

farther

Farther means at a greater distance. The sun is **farther** from us than the moon is.

fast

Fast means quickly. A rocket goes very **fast.**

fat

fat

Fat means big and round. Pigs and hippopotamuses are **fat.**

father

A **father** is a man who has at least one child. **Fathers** and mothers take care of their children.

favorite

Favorite means what you like the most. Holly's **favorite** flavor of ice cream is chocolate.

fear

1. Fear is what you feel when you are afraid. Many people have a **fear** of water, high places, or very small rooms. **2.** To **fear** is to be afraid. Charlie **fears** the water because he doesn't know how to swim yet.

feather

feather

A **feather** is part of a bird. Most birds are covered with them. **Feathers** are light and soft.

February

February is the second month of the year. It has 28 or 29 days. **February** comes after January and before March.

fed

Fed is a form of **feed.** Luisa **fed** her rabbit some lettuce this morning.

feed

To **feed** means to give food to. Russ likes to **feed** the birds in the park. —**fed**

feel

1. To **feel** is to touch. If you have ever **felt** a cat's tongue, you know that it is rough. **2.** To **feel** is also to be some way. When you are happy, you may **feel** like singing. When our friends are sick, we **feel** sorry for them. Ice **feels** cold. —**felt**

feed

feet

Feet means more than one **foot**. People have two **feet**. Dogs and cats have four **feet**. Ken is over four **feet** tall.

fell

Fell is a form of **fall**. Erin **fell** off her bicycle. Ted **fell** asleep.

felt

Felt is a form of **feel**. Yesterday Chris **felt** too sick to go out. The cat's fur **felt** soft when I touched it.

female

Female is a kind of person or animal. It is the opposite of **male**. Girls and women are **female** people.

fence

A **fence** is made to keep two places apart. **Fences** can be made of wood, metal, or stone.

few

Few means not many. Glenn ate a **few** bites of his supper, but he wasn't very hungry.

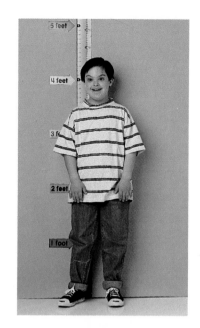

feet

fence

field

1. A **field** is a large, flat area of land. No trees grow there. Farmers grow things in **fields.**
2. A **field** is also where some sports are played. Baseball and football are played on different kinds of **fields.**

field

fight

1. To **fight** is to get mad at someone when you cannot agree. People often shout when they **fight. 2.** A **fight** is what happens sometimes when people do not agree. Ethan and his brother got in a **fight.** —**fought**

fill

To **fill** means to make something full. Ron **filled** two glasses with milk.

fill

find

To **find** is to see where something is. Matt looks around his room for his shoes. He **finds** them under the bed. Yesterday he **found** three socks there. —**found**

fine

Fine means very good. Today is a **fine** day for a walk. Jenny was sick last week, but she feels **fine** now.

103

finger

finger

A **finger** is a part of the hand. People have five **fingers** on each hand. They have ten **fingers** in all.

finish

To **finish** is to come to the end of something. Tino took so much food that he couldn't **finish** it.

fire

Fire is flame, heat, and light. It is what happens when something burns. We cut wood for the **fire** at our camp.

fire

fire engine

A **fire engine** is a kind of truck. **Fire engines** carry hoses and ladders to a fire. Firefighters use them to put out the fire.

firefighter

A **firefighter** is a person who puts out fires. **Firefighters** can work in buildings, in forests, or on boats.

fireplace

A **fireplace** is a safe place to have a small fire inside a house. It is made of stone or metal. A **fireplace** must have a chimney for the smoke to go up.

fireplace

fireworks

Fireworks make light, smoke, and a lot of noise in the sky. **Fireworks** shoot off into the sky on small rockets.

first

First means before all the others. The letter *A* is the **first** letter in the alphabet.

fireworks

fish

1. A **fish** is an animal. Fish live in oceans, lakes, rivers, and ponds. They do not have arms or legs, but they do have tails and can swim very well.
2. To **fish** means to try to catch fish. When people do this, they say they are going **fishing**.
—**fish**

fish

105

fisherman

fisherman
A **fisherman** is someone who fishes. Some **fishermen** work on very large boats. Others use a pole and a hook. —**fishermen**

fist
A **fist** is a hand that is closed tight. Tom and Jenny knocked on the door with their **fists**.

fit
1. To **fit** means to be the right size. Larry's favorite shirt **fitted** him last year, but now he is too big for it. **2.** To **fit** is to put something into a small space. Jeff could not **fit** all of his toys into one box. —**fitted**

fist

five
Five is one more than four. **Five** is written **5.** 4 + 1 = 5.

fix
To **fix** is to make something work again when it is broken. The wheel of Paul's bicycle was bent, but he **fixed** it as good as new.

flag

A **flag** is a piece of cloth with colored shapes on it. Every country has a **flag**. Some **flags** are simple, and others are fancy.

flag

flame

A **flame** is the bright, moving part of a fire. **Flames** are very hot.

flash

To **flash** is to show a bright light for a short moment. A lighthouse **flashes** in the night and the fog so that sailors can find their way.

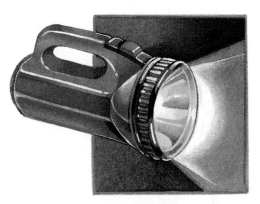

flashlight

flashlight

A **flashlight** is a small lamp that you can carry in your hand. People carry **flashlights** when they go out at night.

flat

Flat means smooth and without any bumps. Floors and tables are **flat**.

flat

flavor

Flavor is what something tastes like. My favorite **flavors** are orange and cherry.

107

flew

Flew is a form of **fly**[1]. The pilot **flew** his airplane over our house.

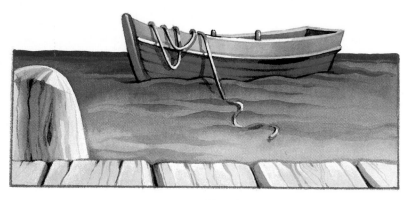

float

float

To **float** is to sit on top of the water. Rob forgot to tie up his boat, and it **floated** away.

flock

A **flock** is a group of sheep. Some dogs know how to keep the **flock** together.

flock

flood

A **flood** is what happens when water comes up over the edges of a river. **Floods** usually come after there is a lot of rain. Sometimes they happen in the spring when the snow melts.

flood

floor

A **floor** is the bottom part of a room. You can walk on the **floor** or lie down on it.

flour

Flour is a white or brown powder. It is made from wheat or potatoes. **Flour** is used to make bread and cake.

flower

A **flower** is part of a plant. Some **flowers** become fruits. **Flowers** come in many colors, shapes, and sizes. People like to smell them and to look at them.

flower

flown

Flown is a form of **fly²**. Nancy goes to visit someone in an airplane every year. She has **flown** to many different cities.

fly¹

fly¹

A **fly** is a kind of insect. It is small and has thin, clear wings. There are many kinds of **flies. —flies**

fly²

To **fly** is to travel through the air. Most birds can **fly**. A pilot **flies** an airplane.
—flies, flew, flown

fly²

109

fog

fog

Fog is a cloud that is near the ground. You cannot see very far in the **fog.**

fold

fold

To **fold** is to bend together. Gail can **fold** paper to make a hat or a bird.

follow

1. To **follow** is to go behind. Elena likes to **follow** her brother around. She **follows** him everywhere he goes.
2. To **follow** also means to come later. March **follows** February every year.

food

Food is what people or animals eat. Lee's favorite **foods** are hamburgers, bananas, and ice cream. Cows eat grass for **food.**

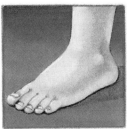  

foot

foot

1. The **foot** is a part of the body. It is at the end of your leg. The toes and the heel are parts of the **foot.** People and birds have two **feet.** Cats and dogs have four **feet. 2.** A **foot** is an amount of length. One **foot** equals 12 inches. —**feet**

football

football

1. Football is a sport. It is played by two teams on a field. One team tries to throw, carry, or kick a ball down the field. The other team tries to stop them. **2.** A **football** is the ball used in a game of football. It has a point at each end.

for

1. For tells why something is there. A carpenter has a box **for** his tools. I bought this book **for** you. **2. For** also means toward. People can reach **for** the sky, but they can't touch it. **3. For** tells how long something continues. We played baseball **for** two hours.

forest

A **forest** is a place with many trees. Many kinds of animals live in **forests**, but few people live there.

forest

forget

To **forget** means not to remember. Joe often **forgets** where he put his shoes. —**forgot, forgotten**

forgot

Forgot is a form of **forget**. Nan **forgot** to put her bicycle in the garage, so it got wet in the rain.

forgotten

Forgotten is a form of **forget**. Ron forgets to bring his lunch to school with him sometimes. He has **forgotten** it twice this week.

fork

fork

A **fork** is a kind of tool to eat with. **Forks** are made of metal or plastic and have sharp points.

form

1. The **form** of something is its shape or what it is like. Clouds have many different **forms. 2.** To **form** something is to give it a shape. Jenny **forms** a piece of clay into a dog. She **formed** another piece of clay into a giraffe. **3.** A **form** is also a kind of something. Ice is another **form** of water. A word can have more than one **form.** *Did* is a **form** of *do.*

forward

Forward means toward the front. Stuart stepped **forward** when his name was called.

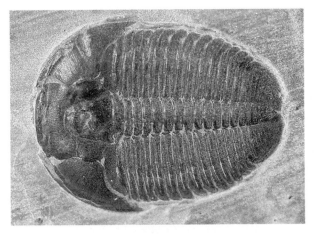

fossil

fossil

A **fossil** is an animal that died a very long time ago and turned to stone. We can see **fossil** dinosaurs today.

fought

Fought is a form of **fight.** Yesterday Don and Bob had a big fight, but today they have forgotten what they **fought** about.

found

Found is a form of **find.** Nick always finds something under his bed. Last night he **found** a baseball bat there.

four

Four is one more than three. **Four** is written **4**. 3 + 1 = **4**.

fox

A **fox** is an animal. It is like a small wild dog. **Foxes** have thick fur, especially on their tails.

fox

free

1. To be **free** means that you can do what you like. Benita doesn't have to go to school today. She is **free** for the whole day. **2.** **Free** also means that you do not have to pay for something. Air and sunlight are **free**.

freeze

To **freeze** is to change from a liquid into something hard. When water **freezes,** it becomes ice. —**froze, frozen**

fresh

1. Fresh means not too old to use. Bread, fruit, and vegetables are best to eat when they are **fresh**. **2. Fresh** air is air that is clean and good to breathe. **3. Fresh** water is water that has no salt in it. There is **fresh** water in rivers, ponds, and lakes.

Friday

Friday is a day of the week. **Friday** comes after Thursday and before Saturday.

fried

Fried is a form of **fry**. Many people like to eat **fried** chicken.

friend

A **friend** is someone you like and who likes you. Molly and Anne play together and share many secrets. They are best **friends.**

friend

friendly

To be **friendly** means to like to meet people. Some animals are **friendly,** but others are not.

frog

A **frog** is a small animal. It has smooth skin, large eyes, and strong back legs. **Frogs** live near water and eat flies.

frog

from

1. **From** means away. Bob was at school. Then he went to the library. Bob went **from** school to the library. **2. From** also means apart. The moon is a long way **from** the earth.

front

Front is the part of something that you see first. Karen's shirt is blue in **front** and has stripes on the back.

front

frost

frost

Frost is water on the ground that freezes into ice. You can see **frost** on windows on cold days.

frown

1. A **frown** is the opposite of a smile. It can tell people that you are not happy, or that you are thinking.
2. To **frown** means to make a frown. Carl **frowned** because he did not know what to do.

frown

froze

Froze is a form of **freeze**. Last night it was so cold that the lake **froze** solid.

frozen

Frozen is a form of **freeze**. Ice is water that has **frozen**.

fruit

fruit

A **fruit** is a part of a plant. It has the seeds of the plant in it. Apples, oranges, and tomatoes are all **fruits.** Many **fruits** are good to eat.

fry

To **fry** is to cook in very hot oil. On Thursdays Jim's father **fries** chicken for the family's supper.
—**fries, fried**

full

Full means that something cannot hold any more. Ken poured juice into his glass until it was **full,** and then he stopped.

fun

Fun is something you like to do. Andy and his friends sang songs and played games at his birthday party. Everybody had a lot of **fun.**

full

117

funny

funny

1. To be **funny** means to make people laugh. Max's uncle tells **funny** jokes. **2. Funny** also means strange. Hana smelled a **funny** smell in the back yard.

fur

Fur is soft, thick hair. Cats, dogs, squirrels, bears, and other animals are covered with **fur**. It keeps them warm in cold weather.

furniture

furniture

Furniture is objects that people sit on, work on, eat on, and sleep on. Chairs, desks, tables, and beds are all **furniture**.

future

The **future** is the part of time that has not happened yet. Tomorrow is in the **future**. Maybe one day in the **future**, people will be living up in space.

ABCDEFGHIJKLMNOPQRSTUVWXYZ
abcdefghijklmnopqrstuvwxyz

gallon

A **gallon** is an amount of a liquid. It is the same as four quarts. Milk and gasoline are sold by the **gallon.**

game

A **game** is a way to play or have fun. Some **games** are played with cards. Others are played with a ball. Every **game** has rules or directions.

gallon

garage

garage

A **garage** is a building where cars and trucks are kept. Many houses have **garages**. A big **garage** in the city can hold hundreds of cars.

garden

A **garden** is a place where plants are grown. People grow flowers and vegetables in **gardens**.

garden

gas

1. A **gas** is something that is so light that it fills up whatever space it is in. Air and steam are **gases**.
2. Gas also means a group of gases that are mixed together to use for cooking or keeping houses warm. Our house has a **gas** stove and **gas** heat. **3. Gas** is also a short way to say **gasoline**.

gasoline

Gasoline is a kind of liquid that can burn. It is burned in cars and trucks to make them go.

gate

A **gate** is a door in a fence. Some **gates** swing in, and others swing out.

gather

To **gather** means to come together or put together. People often **gather** to listen to music. Peter **gathered** up all his toys and put them in one box.

gate

gave

Gave is a form of **give.** Eva gives her father a birthday present every year. Last year she **gave** him a book about space.

geese

Geese means more than one **goose.** In the fall you can watch **geese** flying south for the winter.

get

1. To **get** means to have something come to you. Laura **gets** a pair of socks from her grandmother every year. **2.** To **get** also means to go and take. Helen was hungry, so she went and **got** an apple from the refrigerator. **3.** To **get** can mean to become. Doug **gets** tired from running all the way home. **4.** To **get** means to arrive. The day the bus broke down, everyone **got** to school late. **5.** To **get** up means to stand up. Sometimes Bart falls down, but he always **gets** up again. —**got, gotten**

giant

1. Giant means much bigger than usual. A mouse as big as a horse would be a **giant** mouse. **2.** A **giant** is a very tall person. Many children's stories have **giants** in them.

gift

A **gift** is something that is given. On her birthday, Carol got **gifts** from six of her friends.

gigantic

Gigantic means as big as a giant. We saw **gigantic** rocks when we got to the top of the mountain.

giggle

1. To **giggle** is to laugh in a silly way. Max **giggled** when his father told him a joke. **2.** A **giggle** is a time when you giggle. When Anne heard **giggles** in the closet, she knew her brother was hiding in there.

giant

gift

ginger

Ginger is the root of a plant. It is made into a powder and used in some foods. It is also made into candy and gingerbread.

gingerbread

Gingerbread is a kind of cake. Part of its flavor comes from ginger.

giraffe

A **giraffe** is a large animal. It has long legs and a very long neck. **Giraffes** are covered with brown spots. Their necks are long so that they can eat leaves from the tops of trees.

gingerbread

girl

A **girl** is a female child. **Girls** grow up to be women.

give

To **give** is to let someone else have something. Pedro **gives** his sister a present every year on her birthday.
—**gave, given**

given

Given is a form of **give**. Bud has **given** away some of his toys.

giraffe

glad

Glad means happy. We went to a ball game yesterday. We were **glad** because the weather was good.

glass

1. Glass is what windows are made from. You can see through **glass.** It feels hard, but it is easy to break. Did you know that **glass** is made from sand? **2.** A **glass** is used to hold things. Nick can pour his own juice into a **glass. 3. Glasses** are made to help people see better. **Glasses** are made of glass or plastic. They fit over your nose and in front of your eyes.

glasses

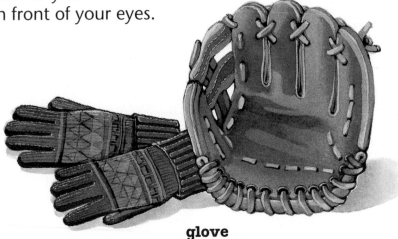

glove

glove

1. A **glove** fits over your hand to protect it. It is made of cloth, wool, leather, or plastic. People usually wear **gloves** to keep their hands warm in cold weather. **2.** Baseball players wear a special kind of **glove** to help them catch the ball. There are many kinds of baseball **gloves.**

glue

Glue is a thick liquid. After it dries, **glue** holds things so they do not come apart.

go

1. To **go** is to move from one place to another. Pam **goes** to school in the morning. She **went** to school late yesterday because the weather was bad. **2.** To **go** also means to leave a place. It is very late, so we have to **go. 3.** To **go** can mean to lead somewhere. The road **goes** through the forest. It **goes** all the way to the city. **4.** To **go** to sleep means to begin sleeping. Harry closed his eyes, but he could not **go** to sleep.
—**goes, went, gone**

goat

A **goat** is an animal on a farm. It has horns and short wool. **Goats** have hair on their chins. **Goats** are raised for their milk and wool.

goat

gold

Gold is a metal. It is soft and yellow. It comes from streams or from underground. **Gold** is used to make rings, coins, and many other things.

goldfish

A **goldfish** is a kind of fish. **Goldfish** are usually small and orange. Many people keep **goldfish** in a bowl at home.

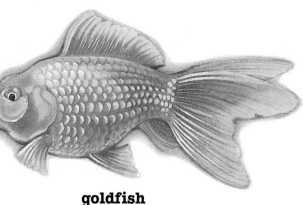

goldfish

gone

Gone is a form of **go.** Sally has **gone** to school. She **went** an hour ago. I came to meet her, but she was already **gone.**

good

1. A thing is **good** when people like it. Chuck's bicycle is easy to ride. It is a **good** bicycle. **2. Good** also means doing things well. Kay's mother is a **good** cook. **3. Good** can also mean that something makes you feel healthy. Cold weather is **good** for penguins.

good-bye

Good-bye is the last thing a person says to another person when they finish talking. Jill said **"Good-bye"** to Carol and then went home.

gooey

To be **gooey** means to stick to everything. Honey sticks to your peanut butter sandwich. It sticks to the spoon you use to get it out of the jar. It sticks to your fingers. Honey is very **gooey.**

goose

goose

A **goose** is a bird. It is like a large duck and has a long neck. Some **geese** fly long distances every winter. —**geese**

got

Got is a form of **get**. Laura **got** socks again for her birthday this year. Beth wanted something to read, so she went and **got** a book from the library. Roseanne almost **got** sick from eating too much. Eddie **got** home late after baseball practice. The next morning he **got** up early to go fishing.

gotten

Gotten is a form of **get**. Laura has **gotten** more socks than she knows what to do with. I offered to get a banana for my sister, but she had already **gotten** one. Kim has never **gotten** too tired to play. Stan had already **gotten** up by seven o'clock.

grade

A **grade** is where you are in school. In her first year Penny was in the first **grade**. This year she is in the second **grade**. There are six **grades** in Penny's school.

grain

1. A **grain** is a seed of wheat, rice, or corn. Flour and cereal are made from many kinds of **grain**. 2. A **grain** also means a very tiny piece. **Grains** of sand are very, very small.

gram

A **gram** is a small amount of weight. A penny weighs almost three **grams**.

grain

grandfather

A **grandfather** is the father of your mother or father. A person can have two **grandfathers**.

grandmother

A **grandmother** is the mother of your mother or father. A person can have two **grandmothers**.

grape

A **grape** is a kind of fruit. It is small and round. **Grapes** are usually larger than berries. **Grapes** are purple or green.

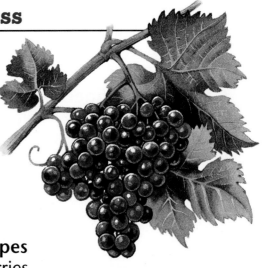

grape

grapefruit

grapefruit

A **grapefruit** is a large, round, yellow fruit. **Grapefruits** are like large oranges, but they are not as sweet.

grass

Grass is a plant. It grows in yards, fields, meadows, and parks. There are many different kinds of **grasses**.

grass

grasshopper

grasshopper

A **grasshopper** is a large insect. It has long, strong back legs. A **grasshopper** can jump many feet in one hop.

gray

Gray is a color. Elephants and rain clouds are **gray.**

great

1. Great means large. There is a **great** old tree in the back yard. **2. Great** also means very important. Alex has pictures of many **great** people. **3. Great** can mean very good. We had a **great** time on our vacation.

green

Green is a color. Leaves and grass are **green** in the summer.

greenhouse

greenhouse

A **greenhouse** is a special building to grow plants in. **Greenhouses** usually have glass roofs. The air inside is always warm.

grew

Grew is a form of **grow**. Dale **grew** tomatoes in the garden last summer. Sharon always wanted to be a teacher, and when she **grew** up that is what she became.

grin

A **grin** is a big smile. Carita cut a **grin** on her pumpkin for Halloween. She likes to cut crooked **grins** because they look funny.

grin

ground

The **ground** is the earth. John fell on the **ground** and hurt his knee. Plants grow out of the **ground.**

group

A **group** is a number of people or things together. A small **group** of students took a trip to the country. Everyone in the **group** had a good time.

group

grow

1. To **grow** is to get bigger. Animals and plants **grow** as they get older. **2.** To **grow** up means to become a woman or a man. When you **grow** up, you may be taller than your father. **—grew, grown**

grown

Grown is a form of **grow**. That tree has **grown** so big that it covers the house.

grownup

A **grownup** is someone who has grown to be a man or a woman. Our parents are **grownups.** Sometimes they want you to act like a **grownup.**

guard

1. To **guard** is to watch something so that nothing bad happens to it. Martha **guarded** the picnic basket so that ants and flies would not get the food. **2.** A **guard** is a person who watches over something. There are always **guards** in front of the palace.

guard

guess

To **guess** is to try to think of the answer. Sally does not know where her cat is. She **guesses** that the cat is up in a tree. When she found the cat in the garage, she knew she had **guessed** wrong.

gym

A **gym** is a place inside a building where people play games and do exercises. Most schools have large **gyms.**

gym

habit

A **habit** is something you do often. George has a **habit** of drinking a glass of water every night before he goes to bed. People can have good **habits** or bad **habits**.

had

Had is a form of **have**. Tom and Lucy have four dollars in their bank. Last month they only **had** two dollars.

hadn't

Hadn't is a short way to say **had not**. James wanted to watch television, but he **hadn't** done his homework yet.

hair

Hair is what grows on your head. Animals and people have **hair**. **Hair** is straight or curly. People can wear their **hair** long or short.

haircut

A **haircut** is when or how your hair is cut. Jackie gets a **haircut** every month.

half

A **half** is one of two pieces that are the same size. Jim cut his sandwich in **half**. Both **halves** were the same. —**halves**

hall

A **hall** is a place inside a building. It leads from one room to another room or rooms. Some **halls** are short and some are long and narrow.

Halloween

Halloween is a holiday. It comes on the last day of October. People wear costumes on **Halloween**. Then they may go out to collect candy in their neighborhood.

haircut

half

Halloween

halves

Halves means more than one **half.** Jim cut a pie into two **halves.**

ham

Ham is a kind of meat. It comes from pigs. You can buy **hams** at the supermarket.

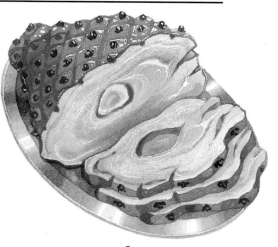

ham

hamburger

1. Hamburger is a kind of beef. It has been cut up in very small pieces so you can make it into different shapes.
2. A **hamburger** is a sandwich. It is made from hamburger and is flat and round. Denise likes to eat **hamburgers** on a roll with onions and ketchup.

hammer

hammer

A **hammer** is a tool. It has a handle and a heavy metal head. It is shaped like a T. **Hammers** are used to hit nails into wood.

hamster

A **hamster** is a small animal. It is covered with short fur and has a short tail. **Hamsters** make good pets.

hamster

134

hand

A **hand** is a part of the body. Your **hands** are at the ends of your arms. People use their **hands** to hold things and to use tools. The fingers, the thumb, and the palm are parts of the **hand.**

handkerchief

A **handkerchief** is a piece of cloth. You put it over your nose when you sneeze. Many **handkerchiefs** are white.

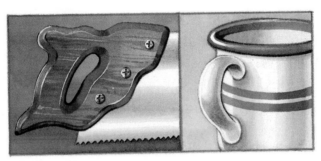

handle

handle

1. A **handle** is a part of something that you can hold with your hand. Cups, suitcases, and tools all have **handles. 2.** To **handle** something is to hold or touch it with your hands. Sharp tools must be **handled** with care.

hang

To **hang** is to be held by something above. Scott can **hang** from a tree with his hands. —**hung**

happen

To **happen** means to take place. Terry told her parents everything that **happened** at camp. What **happens** to the sun at night?

hang

happy

To be **happy** means to feel good. Donna smiled and laughed at the party because she was **happy.**

hard

1. When something is **hard** it is not easy to shape with your fingers. Most rocks are **hard. 2. Hard** is the opposite of easy. Sometimes homework is **hard.**

hardly

Hardly means almost not at all. There were so many clouds that we **hardly** saw the sun all day.

has

Has is a form of **have.** Pete **has** two dollars. Alan **has** two dollars, too. Together they have four dollars.

hat

hat

A **hat** is something you wear on your head. **Hats** come in many different shapes and sizes.

hatch

To **hatch** is to break out of an egg. Baby birds are very small when they **hatch.**

hatch

have

To **have** something means that it is with you. Tom **has** a book in his hand. This morning he **had** two books. Cats **have** soft fur. —has, had

haven't

Haven't is a short way to say **have not**. Maggie and Lynnette **haven't** seen their new baby brother yet.

hawk

A **hawk** is a bird. It has a short, curved beak and strong claws. **Hawks** fly high in the sky and catch small animals on the ground.

hawk

hay

Hay is a kind of tall grass that has been cut and dried. Horses and cows eat **hay**.

hay

he

He means a male person. Edward is a boy. **He** and his brother Fred are twins.

head

1. The **head** is a part of the body. Your face and your ears are parts of your **head. 2.** A **head** also means a part of a tool. It is the heavy part that does the work. Hammers and axes have **heads**.

head

heal

To **heal** is to get better when you are hurt. When you cut your finger, it will **heal** in a few days if you keep it clean.

healthy

Healthy means not sick. Tamiko eats good food so that she will stay **healthy.**

hear

To **hear** is to take in sounds with your ears. Rabbits **hear** well because of their large ears. —**heard**

heard

Heard is a form of **hear.** Dick **heard** a loud noise in the other room.

heart

The **heart** is a part of the body. It is in the center of your chest. The **heart** makes the blood move through your body. We can feel the beat of our **hearts** when we run.

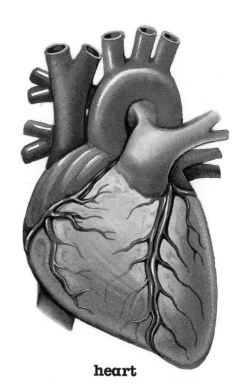

heart

heat

1. **Heat** is what makes things warm. The **heat** from the sun helps plants grow. The **heat** in the oven cooks the food inside it. 2. To **heat** is to make warm. The fire in the fireplace **heated** the whole room up.

heavy

heavy

Heavy means hard to lift. Rocks and bowling balls are **heavy,** but pillows are light.

heel

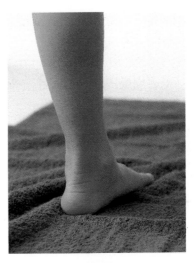

1. The **heel** is a part of the body. It is the back part of the foot. When you put your feet into shoes, your **heels** go in last. **2.** The **heel** is a part of a shoe. It holds up the back of your foot. Some shoes have high **heels.**

heel

height

1. The **height** of something is how high it is. Sandy is five feet tall. Her **height** is five feet. **2.** A **height** is also a high place. Some people are afraid of **heights.**

held

Held is a form of **hold.** Lana lifted the baby and **held** it in her arms. Nick tried to put all his toys in one box, but it only **held** half of them.

helicopter

A **helicopter** is a machine. It carries people through the air. **Helicopters** do not have wings like airplanes. They have propellers on the top. The propeller turns around and lifts the **helicopter** off the ground.

helicopter

hello

Hello is the first word people say to each other when they talk. When people pick up a telephone that is ringing, they usually say "**Hello.**"

help

help

To **help** is to do something together with someone else. The beach umbrella was too heavy for Janet to lift by herself. It was easy when Molly **helped** her.

hen

A **hen** is a bird. Female chickens are **hens**. **Hens** lay eggs.

hen

her

1. Her means a female person. Tom borrowed a book from Rosa. He gave it back to **her** after two days.
2. Her also means belonging to a female person. Jenny has a room in the house where she keeps **her** things. It is **her** room.

here

Here means in this place. We are waiting for the bus, but it is not **here** yet.

hers

Hers means belonging to her. Kip has his own room, and his sister has **hers.** Everything in her room is **hers.**

herself

Herself means her and nobody else. Linda looked at **herself** in the mirror. Then she put on her shoes. Nobody helped her. She put them on by **herself.**

hid

Hid is a form of **hide.** Vic told his sister to hide so that he could look for her. She **hid** behind the house.

hidden

Hidden is a form of **hide.** I found my shoe **hidden** behind the bed.

hide

To **hide** something is to put it where nobody will see it. Sometimes Eric likes to **hide** himself, then jump out and surprise people.
—hid, hidden

hide

high

High means up. There was an eagle flying **high** in the sky. It was up so **high** we could hardly see it. On hot days the temperature is **high**.

hill

A **hill** is a big bump in the ground. You can climb up one side of a **hill** and down the other side. A **hill** is like a small mountain.

hill

him

Him means a male person. On Dean's birthday, his grandfather took **him** to a baseball game.

himself

Himself means him and nobody else. Brad had a mask on his face. When he looked at **himself** in the mirror, he scared **himself**.

hippopotamus

A **hippopotamus** is a large animal. It is as big as a small car. **Hippopotamuses** have short legs and large mouths. They live near lakes or rivers and eat grass.

hippopotamus

his

His means belonging to him. This bicycle belongs to Alex. It is **his** bicycle.

hit

To **hit** is to touch something very hard. Baseball players try to **hit** the ball with a bat. An apple fell from the tree and **hit** the ground. —**hit**

hive

A **hive** is a home for bees. Bees make honey inside of **hives**.

hobby

A **hobby** is something you like to do when you have time. Some **hobbies** are collecting things, drawing, playing music, and inventing things. —**hobbies**

hockey

hockey

Hockey is the name of two sports. In **field hockey** two teams hit a ball across a field with sticks. In **ice hockey** two teams hit a piece of rubber across the ice. **Ice hockey** players wear skates.

hold

1. To **hold** is to have something in your hands or arms. People can **hold** very large things in their arms. They can **hold** small things in their hands. **2.** To **hold** also means to have room for. A small car will only **hold** four people. —**held**

143

hole

A **hole** is an empty place in something. Some birds and animals live in **holes** in trees. The children dug a very deep **hole** in the sand at the beach. Then they filled it back up.

holiday

A **holiday** is a special day. Some people do not have to go to school or work on **holidays**. Sometimes there are parades and fireworks on **holidays**.

hollow

Hollow means with an empty space inside. Basketballs are **hollow**. Some animals live in **hollow** trees.

home

A **home** is a place where people or animals live. Most people have **homes** in houses or apartments.

homework

Homework is work that you bring from school to do at home. The next day you bring it back to school for the teacher to correct.

honest

To be **honest** means to tell the truth. Dan tries to be **honest** so that people will trust him.

hole

hollow

honey

Honey is a thick, sweet liquid. It is made by bees. **Honey** is good to eat on pancakes, in cereal, and with many other foods.

honey

hook

A **hook** is a curved piece of metal. Some **hooks** have points on the end and are used to catch fish. Other **hooks** are used to hang up clothes.

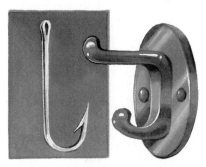

hook

hop

1. To **hop** is to jump up in the air. Rabbits, frogs, grasshoppers, and kangaroos **hop** from place to place.
2. A **hop** is a jump. Amy jumped over the stream in one **hop**. —**hopped**

hope

To **hope** is to believe something good may happen. We want to swim in the lake tomorrow. We **hope** tomorrow will be sunny. Brent **hopes** his mother will cook something good for dinner.

hop

horn

1. A **horn** is part of an animal's body. Bulls and goats have two **horns** on their heads. **2.** A **horn** is also an instrument. Emily blows into her **horn** to make music. **3.** A **horn** can be something that makes a loud noise in the air. We heard the truck's **horn** blow two times.

horn

horse

A **horse** is a large animal with long legs. **Horses** live on farms. People like to ride **horses.**

horseshoe

A **horseshoe** is a piece of iron that is shaped like a U. Horses wear **horseshoes** to protect their feet.

horseshoe

hose

A **hose** is a tube made of rubber or cloth. Firefighters use **hoses** to put water on fires.

hospital

A **hospital** is a large building. Doctors and nurses take care of sick people in **hospitals.**

hose

hot

Hot means able to burn. The sun is **hot** on bright summer days. The inside of an oven is **hot.**

hot dog

A **hot dog** is a kind of food. It is made from meat and other things. People often eat **hot dogs** in long rolls with mustard on them.

hotel

A **hotel** is a big building with many rooms. People who are away from home stay in them. Big cities have many **hotels,** because many people visit the city.

hour

An **hour** is an amount of time. There are 24 **hours** in one day. One **hour** has 60 minutes in it.

house

house

A **house** is a building where people live. When Erica got to her **house,** she was glad to be home.

how

1. How tells the way something is done. Penny wanted to know the way to make a rabbit come out of her hat. "**How** did you make that rabbit come out of your hat?" she asked the magician. He did not tell her **how** he did it. **2. How** much tells the amount of something. **How** much rain did we get yesterday?

hug

hug

To **hug** is to put your arms around something and hold it tight. Many people **hug** each other to show that they are glad to see each other. —**hugged**

huge

Huge means very big. Jim made himself a sandwich with turkey, ham, cheese, lettuce, tomato, and three pieces of bread. This was a **huge** sandwich.

huge

human

Human means about people. A **human** body is the body of a person. Girls and boys and men and women are **human**.

hump

hump

A **hump** is a bump on an animal's back. Some camels have two **humps.** Other camels have one **hump.**

hundred

A **hundred** is a number. It is written **100.** It takes ten tens to make one **hundred.** One **hundred** is ten times ten.

hung

Hung is a form of **hang.** Bart's mother asked him to hang his shirt in the closet. He said he had **hung** it up already.

hungry

To be **hungry** is to want to eat. Betsy has not eaten yet. Her stomach is empty. Betsy is very **hungry.**

hunt

To **hunt** is to look for something. Sam could not find his shoes. He **hunted** for them all over the house. Then he found them behind his desk. Some people **hunt** wild animals.

hurry

To **hurry** is to try to go quickly. When you are late, you have to **hurry.** —**hurries, hurried**

hurt

1. To **hurt** is to break something or make something feel bad. If you fall on the sidewalk, you may **hurt** yourself. **2.** To **hurt** also means to feel bad. Juana's back got burned in the sun when she went to the beach. It got very red and **hurt** for several days. —**hurt**

husband

A **husband** is a married man. He is the **husband** of the woman he married. **Husbands** and wives are married to each other.

hut

A **hut** is a very simple, small house. **Huts** are usually built in places where the weather is warm. Some **huts** are made of grass.

hut

I J
A B C D E F G H **I** J K L M N O P Q R S T U V W X Y Z

a b c d e f g h **i** j k l m n o p q r s t u v w x y z

I

I is a word you use when you speak about yourself. This coat belongs to me. I wear it during the winter to keep me warm.

ice

Ice is water that has frozen. It is hard and cold. Annabel skates on the **ice** that covers the pond. Bill put **ice** in his drink to keep it cold.

ice

ice cream

Ice cream is a kind of food.
It is a frozen dessert.
Ice cream is made from
cream or milk, eggs, and
sugar. **Ice cream** comes
in many different flavors.

ice cream

idea

An **idea** is something that
you think of. You can have
an **idea** about anything.
Max and Scott often get
ideas for new inventions.

if

If asks what might happen. Jack may decide to go
to the store, or he may not. **If** he goes, he will buy
some bread. **If** it rains today, we will need to use our
umbrellas.

igloo

igloo

An **igloo** is a kind of house. It is made of blocks of
snow. People who live in cold places where there are
no trees sometimes build **igloos**.

ill

Ill means sick. Richard is too **ill** to go outside today.

I'll

I'll is a short way to say **I will.** After I finish this book, **I'll** be glad to let you borrow it.

I'm

I'm is a short way to say **I am. I'm** almost as tall as my brother.

ill

imagine

To **imagine** is to see a picture in your mind. When the snow is falling outside her window, Laura likes to **imagine** that it is summer. She **imagines** herself at the beach in the warm sun.

important

Important things are things you care about or need. Tracy will feel bad if she does not learn to ski. It is **important** to her to learn to ski. Teachers and scientists do work that helps other people. They are **important** people.

impossible

Impossible means that something cannot be. It is **impossible** for the sun to come up in the west.

in

1. **In** tells where something is. Fish swim **in** the water.
2. **In** tells when something happens. Ted's birthday is **in** August. We will have dinner **in** one hour.

inch

An **inch** is an amount of length. There are twelve **inches** in one foot.

inch

injure

To **injure** means to hurt. Two people were **injured** in the accident.

ink

ink

Ink is a liquid that people write with. When you write with a pen, **ink** comes out onto the paper. Many pens have blue or black **ink**, but **ink** can also be other colors.

insect

An **insect** is a small animal. All **insects** have six legs. Some **insects** can fly. Flies, ants, butterflies, grasshoppers, and bees are all **insects**, but spiders are not.

insect

inside

1. To be **inside** means to be in something. Donna played outside until she got cold. Then she went **inside** the house to get warm.

2. The **inside** of something is the part that holds things. The **inside** of a baseball has string in it.

inside

instant

An **instant** is a very short amount of time. **Instants** are almost too short to notice. Lightning only flashes for an **instant**.

instead

Instead means in the place of. Melissa wanted to eat an orange. But she only found pears in the refrigerator. So she ate a pear **instead**.

instrument

An **instrument** is something that makes music. Pianos, trumpets, drums, violins, trombones, and xylophones are all **instruments**.

instrument

interest

An **interest** is something you like to learn more about. Elisa has a great **interest** in drawing. She has many other **interests**, too.

interested

To be **interested** in something means to be curious about it. Barry is very **interested** in music.

into

1. Into tells where something goes. My father drives the car **into** the garage. **2. Into** also tells what something becomes when it changes. Caterpillars change **into** moths and butterflies.

invent

To **invent** means to make something that nobody has ever made before. My uncle has **invented** many useful machines.

invention

An **invention** is a thing that someone invents. Wheels, radios, and computers are important **inventions.**

invite

To **invite** is to ask someone to come and visit you. Tina **invited** three of her friends for dinner.

iron

1. Iron is a kind of metal. It is gray or black. **Iron** is very hard and strong. **2.** An **iron** is used to take wrinkles out of clothes. The bottom of the **iron** is flat and gets very hot. Some **irons** make steam.

iron

is

Is is a form of **be.** Last year John was six years old. This year he **is** seven. Next year he will be eight.

island

An **island** is an area of land that has water all around it. Rivers, ponds, lakes, and oceans can all have **islands** in them.

island

isn't

Isn't is a short way to say **is not.** "Is Karen home?" "No, she **isn't.**"

it

1. It means a thing. Tony took his bicycle out of the garage. Then he rode **it** to the store. **2. It** also means the way things are. **It** is raining today. If **it** is cold enough tomorrow, **it** may even snow.

itch

To **itch** is to make you want to scratch. Mel's arm **itches** where the mosquito bit him.

its

Its means belonging to it. Sometimes a dog or cat will chase **its** own tail.

it's

It's is a short way to say **it is.** What a beautiful day it is. **It's** too nice to stay inside.

itself

Itself means it and nothing else. Tom's mother said, "Clean up your room! It won't clean **itself!**"

I've

I've is a short way to say **I have.** I would like to go to the circus. **I've** never been to one before.

A B C D E F G H I J K L M N O P Q R S T U V W X Y Z

a b c d e f g h i j k l m n o p q r s t u v w x y z

jacket

A **jacket** is a short, light coat. **Jackets** are good for spring and fall when the weather is cool.

jail

A **jail** is a kind of building. It has metal poles on the windows and doors. People who break the law have to stay in **jail**.

jacket

jam

Jam is a kind of food. It is made from fruit and sugar boiled together. **Jams** are thick and sweet.

January

January is the first month of the year. It has 31 days. **January** comes after December and before February.

jar

A **jar** is used to hold things. It looks like a fat bottle with a wide top. Many foods come in glass **jars**.

jar

jaw

A **jaw** is a part of the body. It is a bone at the bottom of your face. When you speak, your **jaw** moves.

jelly

Jelly is a kind of food. It is made from fruit juice and sugar boiled together. **Jellies** can be made from many kinds of fruit. —**jellies**

jellyfish

A **jellyfish** is an animal. It has a soft body and floats in the ocean. **Jellyfish** can hurt you if they touch you.

jellyfish

159

jet

jet

A **jet** is a kind of airplane. Its engines do not use propellers. **Jets** fly faster than other planes.

jewel

A **jewel** is a kind of stone. Light can pass through it. Diamonds, emeralds, and rubies are **jewels.** People often pay a lot of money for **jewels.**

job

A **job** is the work someone has to do. It is Wade's **job** to help wash the dishes after supper. When people finish school, they try to get **jobs** to make money. Barbara is a carpenter. That is her **job.** Todd is a writer. That is his **job.**

jog

jog

To **jog** is to run. People who **jog** do not try to run fast. They **jog** for exercise, to make themselves healthy. —**jogged**

jungle

A **jungle** is a place where many trees and large plants grow. **Jungles** are found in places where the weather is warm. Lions, tigers, birds, monkeys, and snakes live in the **jungle**.

junk

Junk is something that people do not want. Old cars and broken furniture are **junk**.

just

1. Just means only. Kim thought she heard a monster outside the window, but it was **just** a squirrel. **2. Just** also means a little before. Jessie's birthday was yesterday. He has **just** turned seven. **3. Just** can also mean the right amount. The kite George wanted cost two dollars. He had two dollars in his pocket. George had **just** enough to buy the kite.

jungle

junk

ABCDEFGHIJ**K**LMNOPQRSTUVWXYZ

abcdefghij**k**lmnopqrstuvwxyz

kangaroo

A **kangaroo** is a large animal. **Kangaroos** move very fast when they jump on their strong back legs. **Kangaroo** mothers carry their babies in a pocket in front of their stomachs.

kangaroo

164

keep

1. To **keep** means to have and not give away. Paula gave Hans a book. She said he could **keep** it as long as he wanted. **2.** To **keep** also means to hold. Mark **kept** his baseball glove in the closet until he needed it. **3.** To **keep** can also mean to be. Kerry has to **keep** quiet while her baby sister is sleeping.
4. To **keep** a promise means to do what you say you will do. Alan said he would come to the party, and he **kept** his promise. —**kept**

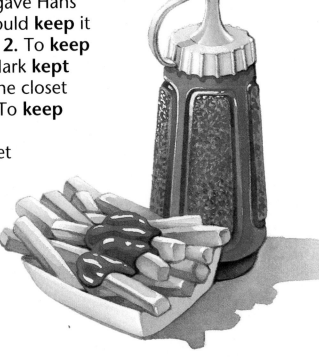

ketchup

kept

Kept is a form of **keep**. Hans **kept** the book for three weeks. Kerry **kept** quiet until her sister woke up.

ketchup

Ketchup is a kind of food. It is a thick, red liquid that is made from tomatoes.

kettle

kettle

A **kettle** is a large pot. Water is boiled in **kettles**.

165

key

1. A **key** is a piece of metal. It opens a lock. People use **keys** to open the doors of their homes and cars.
2. A **key** is also a part of a piano. The **keys** are where you put your fingers to play. There are white **keys** and black **keys** on a piano.

key

keyhole

A **keyhole** is the hole in a lock. You put the key into the **keyhole** and turn it to open the lock.

kick

To **kick** is to hit something with your foot. Bob **kicked** the ball all the way across the field.

kill

To **kill** is to cause something to die. Bad things in the water **killed** the fish.

kick

kilometer

A **kilometer** is an amount of length. One **kilometer** is a thousand meters. A **kilometer** is a little more than half a mile.

kind[1]

Kind means a form of something. Lettuce is one **kind** of vegetable. Carrots and potatoes are other **kinds**.

kind²

To be **kind** is to try to help others. Sara tries to be **kind** to people who have no home.

kindergarten

Kindergarten is a class in school. It is the year before first grade.

king

A **king** is a man who rules a country. He is usually **king** because his father was **king** before him.

kingdom

A kingdom is a place where a king or a queen rules.

kiss

1. To **kiss** is to touch with the lips. Seth **kissed** his mother before he went to bed. **2.** A **kiss** is a touch with the lips. Kelly gives her father a **kiss** when he comes home.

kit

A **kit** is a set of things that you have to put together. Model cars and airplanes often come in **kits.**

kitchen

A **kitchen** is a room in a house where people cook food. A **kitchen** usually has a stove and a refrigerator in it.

kitchen

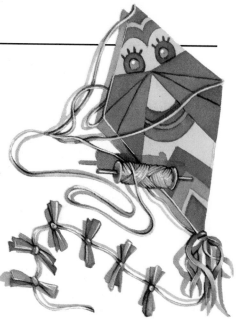

kite

A **kite** is a kind of toy. It is made of sticks covered with paper or cloth. The wind holds a **kite** up in the sky. You hold on to it with a string.

kite

kitten

A **kitten** is a young cat. Most people like **kittens**.

knee

The **knee** is a part of the leg. It bends like an elbow. People bend their **knees** when they sit down.

knew

Knew is a form of **know**. Dana **knew** how to write her name when she was four years old.

kitten

knife

knife

A **knife** is a kind of tool. It has a handle and a piece of metal with a sharp edge. Pete used a **knife** to cut an apple. —**knives**

knight

A **knight** is a person who fights to protect the kingdom of a king or queen. **Knights** lived long ago. Sometimes they wore armor.

knives

Knives means more than one **knife**. **Knives** come in many different sizes and shapes.

knock

To **knock** means to hit. Ellen **knocked** on the door three times before her friend Renee opened it.

knot

A **knot** is a place where two things are tied together. People make **knots** in string, rope, and ribbon.

knight

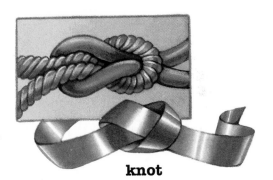

knot

know

1. To **know** someone is to be able to say who they are. Tony **knows** all the teachers in his school. 2. To **know** how means to be able to do something. Bonnie **knows** how to spell *rhinoceros*. —**knew, known**

known

Known is a form of **know**. Al and Sandy have **known** each other for two years. Mark has **known** how to write for a long time.

ABCDEFGHIJK**L**MNOPQRSTUVWXYZ

abcdefghijk|mnopqrstuvwxyz

ladder

A **ladder** is used to climb up and down. It is made of wood, metal, or rope. Firefighters use **ladders** to work in tall buildings.

laid

Laid is a form of **lay**. The carpenter **laid** some boards on the ground. Then he put nails in them.

ladder

lain

Lain is a form of **lie.** Kris likes to lie on his bed. When he has **lain** there for a few minutes, he usually falls asleep.

lake

A **lake** is a large amount of water that is all in one place. A **lake** has land all around it. **Lakes** are not as big as oceans.

lake

lamb

A **lamb** is a young sheep. Wool from **lambs** is very soft.

lamp

A **lamp** is used to make dark places light. Most **lamps** use electricity to make light.

lamb

land

1. Land is the part of the world that is not water. People live on **land. 2.** A **land** is a country. You can collect stamps from many different **lands. 3.** The **land** is the earth or ground that someone uses. The farmers planted potatoes on their **land. 4.** To **land** is to come down to the ground. Dale saw the airplane when it **landed** in a field.

lamp

language

Language is what people use when they speak or write to each other. Some people can speak several **languages.**

large

To be **large** is to fill a lot of space. Elephants are **large** animals.

last

1. **Last** means that there are not any more. The letter *Z* is the **last** letter in the alphabet. 2. **Last** also means the one before. **Last** night it was so cold that there is frost on the ground this morning.

late

Late means after a long time. We got to the movie after it started. We were **late** for the movie. It can get cold outside **late** at night.

later

Later means after more time. We can't come now, but we will see you **later.**

laugh

To **laugh** is to make a sound that shows that something is funny. Greg always **laughs** when he hears a good joke.

laundry

laundry

Laundry is dirty clothes that are ready to be washed. **Laundry** is also clean clothes that have just been washed.

law

A **law** is a rule that people agree to share. **Laws** are made to tell people what is right for them to do.

lay¹

To **lay** is to put something down. When it is time for lunch, a carpenter **lays** down his tools and goes to eat. —**laid**

lay²

Lay is a form of **lie**. Judy was tired. She **lay** down on her bed and went to sleep.

lazy

To be **lazy** is to want to do nothing. Yesterday was so nice that Josh did not want to cut the grass. He felt too **lazy** to work.

lead¹

lead¹

1. Lead is a kind of metal. It is soft and gray. **Lead** is very heavy. **2. Lead** is the part of a pencil that makes marks on the paper. Pencil **leads** are made from a special powder that is pressed together.

lead²

1. To **lead** means to go in front and show the way. Sam **led** his horse into the barn. **2.** To **lead** also means to go. This road **leads** into the forest. —**led**

lead²

leaf

leaf

A **leaf** is part of a plant. **Leaves** are usually green. They are the part that makes food for the plant. **Leaves** come in many different shapes. —**leaves**

learn

To **learn** is to get to know something. Both young people and old people can always **learn** new things.

least

Least means less than any other. A car makes some noise. A bicycle makes less noise. Walking makes the **least** noise of all.

leather

Leather is the skin of some animals. It is made into boots, shoes, and gloves.

leather

leave

1. To **leave** is to go away. We have to **leave** at five o'clock. **2.** To **leave** also means to put something somewhere and then go away. You can **leave** your books on the chair until after dinner. —**left**

leaves

Leaves means more than one **leaf**. All trees have **leaves**.

led

Led is a form of **lead²**. Abby **led** her sister by the hand.

left¹

Left is a direction. It is the opposite of right. We read words on a page from **left** to right.

left²

Left is a form of **leave**. I went to Rolf's house on the way to school, but he had already **left**. Allison cannot remember where she **left** her shoes.

leg

leg

1. A **leg** is a part of the body. Animals and people walk on their **legs**. 2. A **leg** is also a piece that holds something up. Most furniture has **legs**.

lemon

A **lemon** is a kind of fruit. It is yellow. **Lemons** have a sour taste.

lemon

length

Length is how long something is. Our cat's tail is ten inches long. Its **length** is ten inches.

less

Less means not as much. A quart of milk is **less** than a gallon of milk.

let

To **let** means not to stop something. Polly's mother **lets** her have a glass of juice before supper. When Dan threw an apple to his sister, she didn't catch it. She **let** it fall on the ground.

let's

Let's is a short way to say **let us.** "**Let's** go to a movie," Connie said to her father when she came home from school.

letter

1. A **letter** is one of the symbols people use to write words. The **letters** of our alphabet are A, B, C, D, E, F, G, H, I, J, K, L, M, N, O, P, Q, R, S, T, U, V, W, X, Y, and Z. **2.** A **letter** is also a message you write on paper. Eli writes **letters** to all his friends.

letter

lettuce

Lettuce is a kind of vegetable. It has large, green leaves.

lettuce

176

library

library

A **library** is a place where many books are kept. People borrow books from the **library** to take home and read. —**libraries**

lie¹

1. To **lie** is to say something that is not true. When Cindy broke a window, she did not want to get into trouble. So she **lied** and said she had not done it.
2. A **lie** is something you say that is not true. Carlos told his mother a **lie,** but later he decided to tell the truth.

lie²

To **lie** is to be in a place and not move. Our home **lies** at the base of a mountain. Chris **lies** on his bed when he is tired. —**lay, lain**

life

1. Life is what animals and plants have when they are alive. **2.** A **life** is the time something is alive. Insects have short **lives.** Some trees have very long **lives.** —**lives**

lift

To **lift** is to pick up. The rock was so heavy that two people together could not **lift** it.

lift

light¹

1. Light is energy that we can see. The sun, stars, lamps, and candles make **light**.
2. To be **light** is to have **light**. During the day it is **light** outside. **3.** To **light** is to make something burn. Carol **lighted** a fire in the fireplace.

light²

Light means easy to lift. It is the opposite of heavy. Feathers are **light.**

lighthouse

lighthouse

A **lighthouse** is a tall building with a light at the top. **Lighthouses** stand near the shore of the ocean. Their lights flash in the night and fog to tell sailors to keep away.

lightning

Lightning is a big flash of light in the sky. It is a form of electricity. **Lightning** can come from the sky to the ground during storms.

like[1]

To **like** something means that it makes you feel good. Jack and his friends **like** pizza.

like[2]

Like means the same. Brad and Brent are twin brothers. They look just **like** each other.

lime

A **lime** is a kind of fruit. It is green and looks like a small lemon. **Limes** have a sour taste.

line

1. A **line** is a long, thin mark. **Lines** can be straight, curved, or crooked. 2. A **line** is a group of people who are waiting to take turns. Dawn and Mary stood in **line** to buy tickets to a movie.

lightning

lime

179

lion

lion

A **lion** is a large wild animal. It is like a big cat. **Lions** hunt other animals for food. Male **lions** have long, thick hair around their heads.

lioness

A **lioness** is a female lion. **Lionesses** are smaller than male lions. They do not have long hair around their heads.

lip

A **lip** is a part of the face. It is around the outside of your mouth. People have two **lips**.

liquid

A **liquid** is something that you can pour. **Liquid** in a bottle will take the shape of the bottle. Water, milk, and juice are **liquids**.

lip

list

A **list** is a group of names that you write down. Jackie's father gave him a **list** of things to buy at the store. He makes a **list** so Jackie will remember what to buy.

list

listen

To **listen** is to hear and pay attention to. When it started to rain, Gilbert and Matt went home and **listened** to some music.

liter

A **liter** is an amount of a liquid. A **liter** is a little more than a quart.

little

1. **Little** means small. When you were **little,** you could not tie your shoes. 2. A **little** means not very much. Jill ate a **little** soup, but she wasn't very hungry.

live

1. To **live** means to grow and change. Some turtles **live** for more than a hundred years. 2. To **live** means to have a home. Many people **live** in cities. Fish **live** in the water.

lives

Lives means more than one life. Insects have short **lives.**

load

1. A **load** is something to be carried. Phil brought two **loads** of wood into the house.
2. To **load** is to put something in a place where it can be carried away. Liz and her brother **loaded** boxes onto the truck.

load

loaf

A **loaf** is an amount of bread. It is baked in one piece. Tina bought two **loaves** of bread at the store. —**loaves**

loan

To **loan** is to let someone borrow. Pete forgot to bring a pencil, so Carla **loaned** him one of hers.

loaf

loaves

Loaves means more than one **loaf. Loaves** of bread in the store often come already cut in pieces.

lobster

A **lobster** is an animal. It lives on the bottom of the ocean. **Lobsters** have hard shells and big claws and tails.

lobster

182

lock

1. A lock is an object used to keep something shut. You can open the **lock** only if you have a key. **2.** To **lock** means to put the key in the lock and turn it. Arthur **locked** all the doors to his house before he went away.

lock

log

log

A **log** is a large, round piece of wood. **Logs** are cut from trees. Some **logs** are used in fireplaces. Other **logs** are cut up into boards.

long

1. Long is the opposite of short. Swans and giraffes have **long** necks. **2. Long** tells how much time something takes. This television show is one hour **long.**

look

To **look** means to see and pay attention to. Glen and Karen **looked** at all the animals in the zoo.

loose

Loose is the opposite of tight. Mary tried to walk in her mother's shoes, but they were so big that they fell off her feet. The shoes were too **loose** for her.

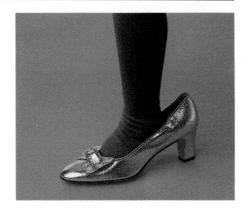

loose

lose

1. To **lose** something is to forget where it is. Becky is always **losing** her gloves. Last winter she **lost** three pairs. **2.** To **lose** a game means that someone else wins. Jason and Mark ran a race to the corner. Jason **lost** the race because he stopped to talk to a friend. —**lost**

lost

Lost is a form of **lose**. Our basketball team only **lost** two games this year.

lot

A **lot** means that something takes a long time to count or measure. There are a **lot** of things to do in the summer. A hippopotamus eats a **lot** of food.

loud

To be **loud** means to make a lot of noise. Thunder in a storm is heard for many miles. Thunder is a **loud** noise.

love

To **love** means to like something very much. Linda **loves** to swim. Derek **loves** to eat sandwiches.

low

1. Low means close to the ground. Nell's little brother has a small chair just for him. It is a **low** chair. **2. Low** also means less than usual. Sometimes vegetables do not cost very much in the summer. Then they have a **low** price.

luck

Luck is something that you do not plan. If you have good **luck,** you may find a quarter on the ground. If your **luck** is bad, your bicycle may get a flat tire.

lumber

Lumber is wood that has been cut into boards. **Lumber** comes from large trees.

lunch

lunch

Lunch is a meal. People eat lunch in the middle of the day. Many people make **lunch** at home and bring it with them to school or work.

lung

A **lung** is a part of the body. You have two **lungs** inside your chest. Air goes in and out of your **lungs** when you breathe.

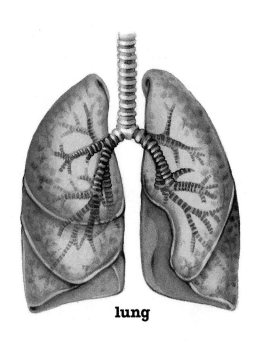

lung

185

ABCDEFGHIJKL **M** NOPQRSTUVWXYZ

abcdefghijkl **m** nopqrstuvwxyz

macaroni

Macaroni is a kind of food. It is made from flour and comes in the shape of little hollow tubes.

machine

A **machine** is an object that does work for people. It may be large or small and may have many parts. Airplanes, computers, and windmills are all **machines**.

machine

mad

Mad means angry. Bill slept too late this morning. Now he is **mad** at himself because he missed the bus to school. —**madder, maddest**

made

Made is a form of **make**. Dale **made** breakfast for his family this morning. Cooking **made** him feel good.

magic

Magic is the power to make impossible things seem real. The wizard changed the prince into a frog by **magic**. Buck learned to do **magic** tricks.

magician

A **magician** is someone who works magic. **Magicians** often pull rabbits out of hats and make things disappear.

magnet

A **magnet** is a piece of metal that iron will stick to. **Magnets** are used in many machines. Kenny stuck a picture on the refrigerator with a **magnet**.

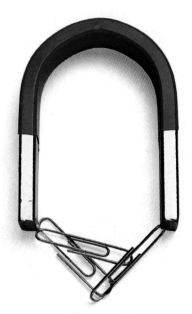

magnet

mail

1. The **mail** is the way we send letters and packages from one place to another. **2.** To **mail** something is to send it through the mail. Alex's parents **mailed** him a package at camp last week.

187

main

Main means most important. A **main** street is large and holds many cars.

make

make

1. To **make** means to cause to be. Wes can use flour, water, butter, and apples to **make** a pie. Good music **makes** Franco feel happy. **2.** To **make** a bed means to fold the edges of the blanket under the mattress. Melanie **makes** her bed every morning. **3.** To **make** money is to get money. Don **made** a dollar helping his father. —**made**

male

Male is a kind of person or animal. It is the opposite of female. Boys and men are **male** people.

man

A **man** is a grown male person. Boys grow up to be **men.** —**men**

many

Many is a large number or amount. There are very **many** grains of sand on the beach.

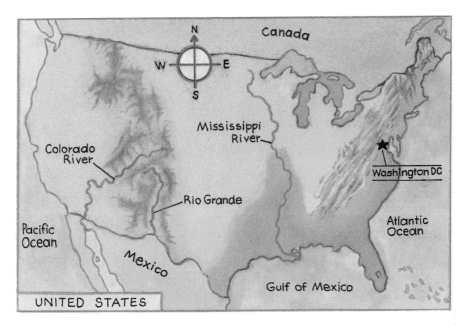

map

map

A **map** is a picture that shows where places are. **Maps** can show countries, cities, towns, roads, rivers, lakes, mountains, and many other things.

maple

A **maple** is a kind of tree. **Maple** trees turn beautiful colors in the fall.

maple

marble

1. Marble is a kind of stone. It is used to make statues and buildings. Most **marble** is white, but it can also be pink or gray or other colors.
2. A **marble** is a small glass ball. **Marbles** are used in several games.

marble

189

march

To **march** with someone means to take the same size steps at the same time. Our band **marched** in the parade.

March

March is the third month of the year. It has 31 days. **March** comes after February and before April.

march

mark

1. A **mark** is a spot you can see on something. Pens and pencils leave **marks** on paper. **2.** To **mark** is to put a mark on something. The teacher **marked** the right and wrong answers on our tests.

marry

To **marry** someone is to agree to share your lives together. When men and women are **married,** they are husbands and wives. —**marries, married**

marsh

marsh

A **marsh** is an area of land that is soft and wet. Frogs, water birds, and mosquitoes live in **marshes.**

marshmallow

Marshmallow is a kind of candy. It is soft and white. **Marshmallows** are pieces of this candy. They are good to eat.

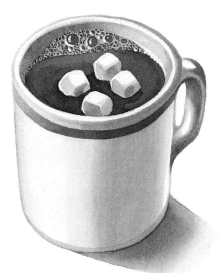

marshmallow

mask

A **mask** is something to cover the face. It can be made of paper, cloth, plastic, or rubber. Dennis wore a red and yellow **mask** with his costume on Halloween.

match

To **match** is to be the same. Janet's shirt and shoes are the same color. She bought the shoes because they **matched** the shirt.

mattress

A **mattress** is the soft top part of a bed. People sleep on **mattresses.**

mask

may

1. May means that there is a chance something will happen. It **may** snow today. It **might** have snowed yesterday, but it didn't. **2. May** also means that nobody will stop you. Larry's mother said he **may** go to the store. **—might**

May

May is a month of the year. It has 31 days. **May** comes after April and before June.

maybe

Maybe means that something may be. **Maybe** Jamie will come to visit us this afternoon.

me

Me is a word I use when I speak about myself. After I bought the kite, it belonged to **me.** My grandmother sent **me** a puzzle for my birthday.

meadow

meadow

A **meadow** is an area of land that is covered with long grass. Mice, rabbits, and butterflies live in **meadows.**

meal

A **meal** is an amount of food that people eat at one time. Breakfast, lunch, and dinner are **meals.**

meal

mean¹

1. To **mean** is to say the same thing as. Large is another word for big. Large and big **mean** the same thing. **2.** To **mean** is also to be important. Allison wants very much to go to the movies. It **means** a lot to her. —**meant**

mean²

To be **mean** is not to be friendly or kind. **Mean** people are not nice to be with.

meant

Meant is a form of **mean.** Did you understand what I **meant?** Going to the movies **meant** a lot to Allison.

measure

measure

To **measure** is to find out how big something is. You can **measure** some things in inches, feet, or meters. Liquids can be **measured** in quarts or liters.

meat

Meat is a kind of food. It comes from animals. Chicken, beef, and ham are all **meats.**

medicine

Medicine helps sick people get well. Many **medicines** are made from plants. Usually a doctor tells you what kind of **medicine** to take.

meet

1. To **meet** is to get to know someone. You **meet** many new people on the first day of school.
2. To **meet** also means to be at the same place at the same time. Dan and Bill **met** at the corner at three o'clock. —**met**

melt

To **melt** is to change from something solid into a liquid. When the weather gets warm, ice **melts** and becomes water.

memory

Memory is what makes people able to remember. If you have a good **memory**, you can remember a lot of things.

melt

men

Men means more than one **man**. Boys grow up to be **men**.

mess

A **mess** is something that is not neat. Leslie's room had clothes, toys, and books all over the place. She had not made her bed, either. The room was such a **mess**, her mother told her her to clean it up.

mess

message

A **message** is a group of words that is sent from one person to another. Many people send **messages** through the mail.

met

Met is a form of **meet**. Pia **met** six new friends at the school picnic. Ann and Barbara **met** to have lunch at a restaurant.

metal

A **metal** is something that comes from the ground. **Metals** can bend and not break. Iron, gold, silver, copper, and lead are all kinds of **metal**.

meter

meter

A **meter** is an amount of length. One **meter** is a little more than a yard. There are 1,000 **meters** in a kilometer.

mice

Mice means more than one **mouse**. Our cat is afraid of **mice**.

microscope

A **microscope** is used to see things that are too small to see with our eyes alone. **Microscopes** can make tiny things look big.

microscope

middle

The **middle** of something is the inside. It is not close to the ends. Your elbow is in the **middle** of your arm.

midnight

Midnight is the middle of the night. It comes at 12 o'clock at night.

might

Might is a form of **may.** Our friends **might** have come to see us last night, but we don't know because we were not home.

mile

A **mile** is an amount of distance. There are 5,280 feet in a **mile.** It takes a man or woman about 20 minutes to walk a **mile.**

milk

Milk is a kind of food. It is a liquid that comes from cows, goats, and other animals. **Milk** can be made into butter and cheese.

milk

million

A **million** is a number. It is written 1,000,000. There are a thousand thousands in a **million.** The sun is **millions** of miles away from the earth.

mind

The **mind** is the part of a person that thinks, feels, learns, remembers, wishes, and imagines. Without **minds** humans would not be humans.

mine

Mine means belonging to me. After I bought the book, it was **mine.**

minus

Minus means taken away. If you take two away from six, you have four. Six **minus** two is four. Six **minus** two can also be written 6 – 2.

minute

A **minute** is an amount of time. One **minute** has 60 seconds in it. There are 60 **minutes** in one hour.

mirror

mirror

A **mirror** is a piece of glass you can see yourself in. Darleen looked at herself in the **mirror.**

miss

1. To **miss** means not to hit or catch. Wade swung his bat, but he **missed** the ball. **2.** To **miss** also means to wish something were there when it is not. Sarah had fun on her vacation, but she **missed** her friends at home.

Miss

Miss is a word people use with a woman's name if she is not married. Our music teacher's name is **Miss** Brown.

mistake

A **mistake** is something you do that is wrong. Everyone makes **mistakes.**

mix

To **mix** is to put two or more things together. Tom **mixed** flour, eggs, milk, sugar, and chocolate together in a bowl. Then he baked a cake.

mix

model

A **model** is a small copy of a larger object. Marcus built three **models** of planes. Each **model** was a foot long.

moment

A **moment** is a very small amount of time. If you will wait just a **moment,** I will help you as soon as I can.

model

Monday

Monday is a day of the week. **Monday** comes after Sunday and before Tuesday.

money

Money is what people use to buy things. When people work, they are paid **money** for what they do. Pennies, nickels, dimes, quarters, and dollars are all kinds of **money**.

money

monkey

A **monkey** is a kind of animal. It has long arms and legs and a long tail. Most **monkeys** live in trees. Some **monkeys** have faces and hands that are a lot like the ones people have.

monster

A **monster** is a huge, terrible animal or person. Rex was afraid that there was a **monster** in his closet.

monkey

month

A **month** is a part of the year. There are 12 **months** in the year. They are January, February, March, April, May, June, July, August, September, October, November, and December.

mood

A **mood** is the way you feel. When the weather is bad, Jack is in a bad **mood**.

moon

The **moon** is a big, bright object in the sky. The **moon** goes around the earth. It is very far away.

moon

more

1. More is the opposite of less. There is **more** water in the ocean than there is in a pond.
2. To do **more** means to keep going. Ned ate a sandwich. Then he ate another one. He ate **more** because he was hungry.

morning

Morning is the first part of the day. The sun rises in the **morning.**

morning

mosquito

A **mosquito** is a kind of insect. It is very small and has wings. **Mosquitoes** bite people and animals. **Mosquito** bites itch.
—mosquitoes

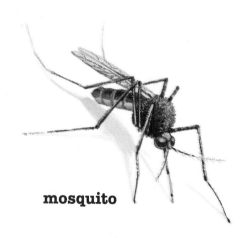

mosquito

most

Most means more than any other. A bicycle makes some noise. A car makes more noise. A train makes the **most** noise of all.

moth

A **moth** is a kind of insect. **Moths** look a lot like butterflies. A caterpillar changes into a **moth** inside a cocoon.

moth

mother

A **mother** is a woman who has a child. **Mothers** and fathers take care of their children.

motor

1. A **motor** is a machine. It uses energy from electricity to do work. Refrigerators use **motors** to keep things cold.
2. **Motor** is also another word for engine.

motorcycle

motorcycle

A **motorcycle** is a machine. It is like a big, heavy bicycle with an engine. Some **motorcycles** can go as fast as cars.

mountain

A **mountain** is an area of land that is higher than the land around it. The tops of very high **mountains** are covered with snow.

mountain

201

mouse

mouse

A **mouse** is a very small
animal. It has a long tail,
short fur, and sharp teeth.
Mice live in fields, forests,
or houses. —**mice**

mouth

The **mouth** is a part of the
head. It is under your nose.
People and animals eat
food with their **mouths**.

mouth

move

1. To **move** is to go from one place to another. Plants
cannot **move** by themselves, but animals can.
2. To **move** also means to go to live in another place.
Del's family **moved** to a new city last year.

movie

A **movie** is a story made with pictures that move.
Moving pictures are made with a special camera.
People watch **movies** in theaters or on television.

Mr.

Mr. is a word people use with a man's name. Our
teacher in the first grade was **Mr.** Bishop.

Mrs.

Mrs. is a word people use with a woman's name if she is married. **Mrs.** Smith took her children to the circus.

Ms.

Ms. is a word people use with a woman's name.
Ms. Cook drives a bus for the city.

much

1. **Much** means a lot. There is not very **much** food in the refrigerator. 2. How **much** tells the amount or cost of something. "How **much** is that basketball?" David asked.

mud

Mud is wet dirt. Many animals like to roll in the **mud**.

mud

multiply

To **multiply** is to add a number to itself several times. The symbol for **multiply** is x. 2 x 4 is the same as 2 + 2 + 2 + 2.
—**multiplies, multiplied**

muscle

A **muscle** is a part of the body. **Muscles** are under the skin. People and animals use **muscles** to move around.

museum

A **museum** is a place where things are collected so that people can go to look at them. **Museums** can have art, machines, models of animals, and many other things.

mushroom

A **mushroom** is a kind of plant. It grows in dark, damp places. Some **mushrooms** look like little umbrellas.

music

Music is sounds that people make with instruments and their voices. There are many kinds of **music** all over the world.

mushroom

must

1. **Must** means that you have to do something. You **must** put a string on your kite, or it will fly away.
2. **Must** also means probably. That book **must** be around here somewhere.

mustard

Mustard is a kind of food. It is yellow or brown and has a strong, hot taste. People like **mustard** on hot dogs and in sandwiches.

my

My means that something belongs to me. This is **my** bicycle.

myself

Myself means me and nobody else. When I look in a mirror, I see **myself**.

mystery

A **mystery** is something that you do not understand. Pam does not understand why plants grow. It is a **mystery** to her. Nature is full of **mysteries**.
—**mysteries**

A B C D E F G H I J K L M N O P Q R S T U V W X Y Z

a b c d e f g h i j k l m n o p q r s t u v w x y z

nail

1. A **nail** is a piece of metal. It has a point at one end. Carpenters use hammers to hit nails into wood.
2. A **nail** is also a part of the body. It is the hard part at the end of your fingers and toes. Sally's mother often tells her not to bite her **nails**.

nail

name

A **name** is a word that people use to call something by. Everything has a **name**. People have **names**, too.

narrow

narrow

Narrow is the opposite of wide. The boards on our fence are close together. There is only a **narrow** space between them.

nature

Nature is everything in the world that is not made by people. Animals, plants, the land, the ocean, the sky, and the weather are all parts of **nature.**

near

To be **near** means to be a small distance away from. Nell can walk from her house to school in two minutes. Her house is **near** the school.

neat

Neat means clean and with everything in place. Linda likes to keep her room **neat.**

neck

The **neck** is a part of the body. It is between your head and your shoulders. Giraffes have long **necks.**

need

To **need** means that you must have something. Plants cannot live without water. They **need** water to live.

needle

1. A **needle** is a kind of tool. It is a very thin piece of metal with a sharp point. **Needles** and thread are used to sew cloth. **2.** A **needle** is a kind of leaf. It is thin and shaped like a sewing needle. Some kinds of trees have **needles.**

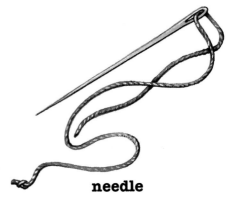

needle

neighbor

neighbor

A **neighbor** is someone who lives near you. Many **neighbors** are friends.

neighborhood

A **neighborhood** is an area where neighbors live. Kim knows almost everyone in his **neighborhood.**

neither

Neither means not either. Teresa went **neither** left nor right. She kept walking straight up the street.

nest

A **nest** is what birds build. Birds lay eggs and feed their babies in **nests. Nests** are made from grass, mud, sticks, string, and other things.

net

A **net** is a kind of bag made of string or rope. Fishermen often use large **nets** to catch fish.

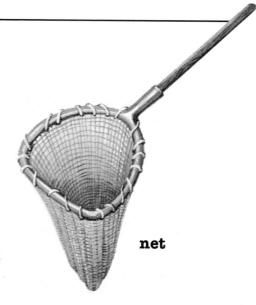

net

never

Never means not ever. The sun always rises in the east. It **never** rises in the west.

new

New is the opposite of old. Alisa's bicycle just came from the store. Nobody ever owned it before. It is a **new** bicycle.

news

The **news** is a story about things that are happening. Many people watch the **news** on television. Other people read the **news** in a newspaper.

newspaper

A **newspaper** is several large pieces of paper with stories and pictures on them. People read the news in a **newspaper**. Many **newspapers** are printed every day.

newspaper

next

Next means the one after this one. This summer Ed stayed at home. **Next** summer he will be able to go to camp.

nice

To be **nice** is to make people feel good. Yesterday the weather was so **nice** that Leah played outside. Our neighbors are **nice**, friendly people.

nickel

nickel

A **nickel** is a kind of coin. One **nickel** is the same as five pennies. Five **nickels** are the same as a quarter.

night

Night is the time when it is dark outside. Most people sleep at **night**.

nightmare

A **nightmare** is a very bad dream. Karen had a **nightmare** after she saw a movie that scared her.

night

nine

Nine is a number. **Nine** is written **9**. $8 + 1 = 9$.

no

1. **No** means that you do not agree. Maureen asked if she could have another dessert. Her mother said, "**No.**"
2. **No** also means not any. There is **no** snow during the summer. Peter was sick yesterday, and he is still sick today. He feels **no** better today than he did yesterday.

nobody

Nobody means no person. **Nobody** can fly like a bird.

nod

To **nod** is to move your head up and down. People often **nod** to show that they agree. —**nodded**

noise

A **noise** is a sound. Many machines make a lot of **noise.**

noon

Noon is the middle of the day. It comes at 12 o'clock. People usually eat lunch around **noon.**

north

North is a direction. If you look where the sun rises, **north** is on your left.

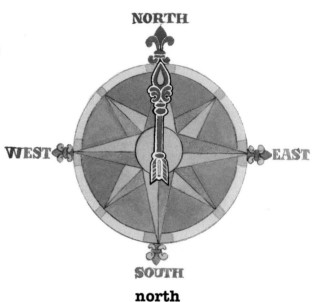

north

nose

The **nose** is a part of the face. It is below your eyes and above your mouth. People and animals smell with their **noses.**

not

The sun shines on us during the day. It does **not** shine on us at night.

nose

note

note

1. A **note** is one sound in music. Music is made of many **notes.** The **notes** can be written down so that other people can read them and play the same music. **2.** A **note** is also a short message that you write down.

nothing

Nothing means no thing. An empty box has **nothing** in it.

notice

To **notice** is to see or hear something. Jill **noticed** that her brother had on two socks that did not match.

November

November is a month of the year. It has 30 days. **November** comes after October and before December.

now

Now means at this time. You are reading these words **now.**

number

1. A **number** is a symbol people use when they count things. One, six, ten, 52, and 100 are all **numbers. 2.** A **number** is also what you use to call people on the telephone. Kelly's **number** is 555-1324.

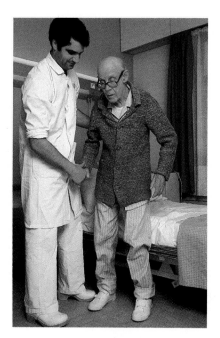

nurse

nurse

A **nurse** is a person who takes care of sick people. **Nurses** work with doctors. Many **nurses** work in hospitals.

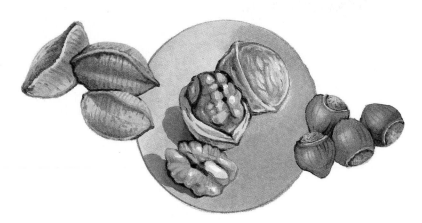

nut

nut

A **nut** is a seed or a dry fruit. It has a hard shell. Many **nuts** grow on trees.

ABCDEFGHIJKLMN O PQRSTUVWXYZ

abcdefghijklmn o pqrstuvwxyz

oak
An **oak** is a kind of
tree. Acorns grow
on **oak** trees.

object
An **object** is anything
that people can see
or touch that is not
alive. Buildings,
tables, chairs, books,
scissors, pens, and
pencils are all
objects.

oak

ocean

ocean

An **ocean** is a very large area of water. **Ocean** water has salt in it. **Oceans** cover almost three quarters of the earth.

o'clock

O'clock is a word people use to say what time it is. Nikos gets up at seven **o'clock** in the morning.

October

October is a month of the year. It has 31 days. **October** comes after September and before November.

odd

1. An **odd** number is a number that you cannot get to when you count by twos. One, three, five, seven, and nine are **odd** numbers. **2. Odd** means strange. Jeff noticed an **odd** smell in the yard. He could not tell what was making it.

of

1. Of means from. Most tables are made **of** wood. **2. Of** also tells what something has in it. Paul was carrying a pail **of** water. **3.** When you tell time, **of** means before. The time is ten minutes **of** four.

off

1. Off is the opposite of on. Our house is dark when the lights are **off. 2. Off** also means away from. Please take your books **off** the table before supper.

offer

To **offer** is to say you will give or do something. Janet **offered** to help her father rake the leaves.

office

office

An **office** is a place where people work. Many people have jobs in **offices.**

often

Often means many times. It **often** rains in April.

oil

Oil is a liquid. It floats on water. **Oils** from vegetables are used in foods. **Oil** from the ground is used in cars and machines.

oil

old

1. Old is the opposite of new. Billy puts on his **old** jacket when he goes out to play football. **2.** To be **old** means to have been alive a long time. My grandmother is **old,** but she still walks a mile every day. **3. Old** tells how long something has been alive. Some trees are thousands of years **old.**

on

1. On is the opposite of off. The room is bright when the light is **on. 2. On** tells where something is. The dishes are **on** the table. **3. On** means about. Thea has a book **on** dinosaurs. **4. On** also tells what day something happens. We play ball **on** Sundays.

once

1. Once means one time. Birthdays only come **once** every year. **2. Once** also means after. **Once** Gary was in the third grade, he had homework to do every night.

one

1. One is a number. **One** is written **1. One** is the first number when you count. **2. One** is used for something you have already talked about. Sarah likes green grapes, but she doesn't like purple **ones.**

onion

An **onion** is a kind of vegetable. It is round and has a strong smell and taste. **Onions** grow in the ground.

onion

only

Only means one and no more. There is **only** one moon in our sky.

open

Open is the opposite of close. Maggie **opened** a jar to get the peanut butter out. The store **opens** at nine o'clock.

opposite

1. **Opposite** means different in every way. Up is the **opposite** of down. 2. To be **opposite** also means to be at either end of a line. East and west are **opposite** directions.

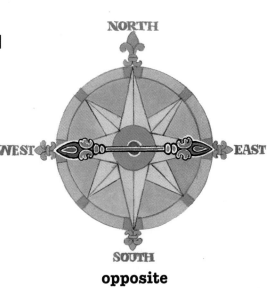

opposite

or

Or shows that you can choose one of two or more things. You can have a turkey sandwich **or** a ham sandwich.

orange

1. An **orange** is a kind of fruit. It is about the size of a tennis ball. **Oranges** grow on **orange** trees.
2. **Orange** is a color. Pumpkins and oranges are **orange**.

orange

orchestra

An **orchestra** is a large group of people who play instruments together. **Orchestras** can have more than a hundred people.

orchestra

order

Order is the way one thing follows another. The letters of the alphabet always come in the same **order**.

ostrich

An **ostrich** is a very large bird. It has long legs and a long neck. **Ostriches** cannot fly.

other

1. **Other** means one of two. One of Vicki's socks has a hole in it. The **other** one has no holes. 2. **Other** also means different. Keiko has no time to play today. She will have time some **other** day.

ostrich

ounce

An **ounce** is an amount of weight. There are 16 **ounces** in one pound.

our

Our means belonging to us. These are **our** clothes. The people who live next door are **our** neighbors.

ours

Ours means belonging to us. Those are your books. These are **ours**.

ourselves

Ourselves means us and nobody else. When Alan and I looked in a mirror, we saw **ourselves** there.

out

Out is the opposite of in. A bird flew in one window and **out** the other. Joe went **out** the door and closed it behind him.

outside

Outside is the opposite of inside. Leo stayed **outside** until it was dark. Then he went into the house. Eggs are smooth on the **outside**.

oval

An **oval** is a shape. It looks like a circle that has been stretched. Hens' eggs are shaped like **ovals**.

oven

An **oven** is a metal box that food is cooked in. Ralph put cookies in the **oven** to bake.

oval

oven

over

1. Over means above. A helicopter flew **over** our house. **2. Over** also means on top of. Jackie wore a sweater **over** her shirt. **3. Over** can also mean more than. Lily's father is **over** six feet tall. **4. Over** can also mean down. Paula knocked **over** a glass of milk. **5. Over** also means again. The band played a song. Then they played it **over** because everyone liked it. **6. Over** can mean finished. After the movie was **over**, we went home.

owe

To **owe** means that you must give someone something. Todd **owes** the store a quarter for his apple.

owl

owl

An **owl** is a kind of bird. It has a large head and large round eyes that look straight ahead. **Owls** come out to hunt at night.

own

To **own** means to have and keep something. Jane **owns** a lot of books and toys.

P p

ABCDEF**G**HIJKLMNO**P**QRSTUVWXYZ

abcdefghijklmno**p**qrstuvwxyz

pack
To **pack** is to put something in a suitcase or a box to take with you. Walter **packed** his clothes and some books to go on vacation.

package
A **package** is something you tie up and send through the mail. People bring **packages** to the post office to mail.

pack

page

A **page** is a piece of paper. There are words on both sides of this **page.** Books are made of many **pages** held together.

paid

Paid is a form of **pay.** Milo **paid** four dollars for a movie ticket.

pail

A **pail** is used to hold things. It is made of metal or plastic and has a flat, round bottom. **Pails** are the same thing as buckets.

pail

pain

Pain is what you feel when you are hurt. If you eat too fast you might get **pains** in your stomach.

paint

1. **Paint** is a liquid with color in it. People put **paint** on things to make them look good. Artists make pictures with **paints.**
2. To **paint** is to cover with paint. Sally and her mother **painted** one room yellow and one room blue.

paint

pair

A **pair** is two things that match each other. Shoes, socks, and gloves come in **pairs**.

pajamas

Pajamas are a kind of clothes that people wear when they sleep. Most **pajamas** are warm and soft.

palace

A **palace** is a huge building where kings and queens live. Some **palaces** have over a hundred rooms.

palm

The **palm** is the inside part of the hand. There are many lines on the **palms** of our hands.

pan

A **pan** is something to cook in. It is made of metal. Our kitchen is full of pots and **pans**.

pancake

A **pancake** is a kind of food. It is a thin, flat cake. **Pancakes** are made of flour, eggs, and milk that you mix together and cook in a hot pan.

pair

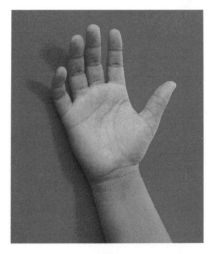

palm

pancake

pants

Pants are a kind of clothes. People wear **pants** over their legs. Most **pants** have pockets in the sides.

paper

Paper is something people use to write on. It is made from wood. Books and newspapers are made of **paper.**

parade

A **parade** is a group of people who march together down the street. Most **parades** have bands that play music as they march. **Parades** often happen on holidays.

parade

parent

A **parent** is a mother or father. Men and women who have children are **parents.**

park

1. A **park** is a place where people can go to enjoy being outside. Most **parks** are full of grass and trees. People in cities like **parks** because they do not have land of their own.
2. To **park** is to put a car somewhere and leave it there. Ned's father **parks** the car in the garage every night.

park

parrot

A **parrot** is a kind of bird. It has a large beak and feathers in bright colors. Some **parrots** can learn to say a few words.

parrot

part

A **part** is one piece of something. Leaves, branches, roots, and the trunk are **parts** of a tree.

party

A **party** is a time when people get together to have fun. Many people have a **party** on their birthday. —**parties**

pass

1. To **pass** means to go past. Cars **pass** each other on the left. **2.** To **pass** also means to give to someone with your hands. Brianna **passed** the bread to her father at the table. **3.** To **pass** a test means to do well. Neil **passes** most of his tests in school.

party

past

1. The **past** is the part of time that has already happened. Yesterday is in the **past**. **2.** To go **past** means to go beside. A big river goes **past** many towns and cities.

patch

1. A **patch** is a small piece of cloth. People sew **patches** on clothes to cover up holes. **2.** A **patch** also means an area of ground. The farmer grew pumpkins in his pumpkin **patch.**

patch

path

A **path** is a place where you can walk through a field or a forest. Dave and his friends followed a **path** to the lake.

paw

paw

A **paw** is the foot of some animals. Dogs, cats, bears, and rabbits all have four **paws.**

pay

1. To **pay** is to give money for something. Louise **paid** two dollars for a book. **2.** To **pay** attention means to look and listen carefully. Philippe **pays** attention when the news comes on the television. —**paid**

pea

A **pea** is a kind of vegetable.
It is small, round, and green.
Peas are the seeds
of **pea** plants.

peace

Peace is a time when
things are quiet. When
the war was over,
everyone was glad
to have **peace.**

pea

peach

A **peach** is a kind of fruit. It is yellow and red and has
a lot of juice inside. **Peaches** grow on trees.

peanut

A **peanut** is a kind of
food. It comes
in a shell and looks
and tastes like a nut.
Peanuts grow in the
ground.

peanut butter

Peanut butter is
a kind of food that is
made from peanuts.
It is soft and smooth.
I like **peanut butter**
sandwiches.

peanut

pear

A **pear** is a kind of fruit. **Pears** are yellow, green,
brown, or red. They are round at both ends, but
one end is smaller than the other.

227

pen

pen

A **pen** is a tool to write with. **Pens** are filled with ink. They are usually made of plastic or metal.

pencil

pencil

A **pencil** is a tool to write with. **Pencils** are made of wood or plastic. The part that writes on paper is called the lead.

penguin

A **penguin** is a kind of bird. It lives near the ocean in places where it is very cold. **Penguins** cannot fly, but they can use their wings to swim in the water.

penguin

penny

A **penny** is a coin. It is the smallest amount of money. One **penny** is one cent. There are 25 **pennies** in a quarter and 100 **pennies** in one dollar. —**pennies**

penny

people

People means more than one **person.** No two **people** are the same.

pepper

Pepper is a kind of food. It comes as small black grains that are made into a fine powder. **Pepper** has a hot taste.

perfect

Perfect means that everything is just right. Todd did a **perfect** job cleaning his room.

perhaps

Perhaps means maybe. **Perhaps** we will have time for a walk after dinner.

person

A **person** is a man, woman, boy, or girl.

pet

A **pet** is a small animal that lives with people. Many people have dogs, cats, or hamsters as **pets.**

phone

phone

Phone is another name for **telephone.** Jen called her friend Carl on the **phone.**

piano

A **piano** is an instrument. It has 88 white and black keys. You push down on the keys with your fingers to make music.

piano

pick

1. To **pick** means to take something off a tree. Bonnie **picked** enough apples to make a pie. 2. To **pick** also means to choose. Stu **picked** out a pair of socks to go with his shirt.

picnic

A **picnic** is a meal that people eat outside. Ants like **picnics** as much as people do.

picnic

picture

1. A **picture** is something you draw or paint. Jeff drew a **picture** of his house. 2. A **picture** can also come from a camera. Many people like to take **pictures** on their vacations.

pie

A **pie** is a kind of food. It is baked in the oven. The outside of a **pie** is often made with flour and butter. The inside can be fruit, cheese, meat, or other things.

pie

piece

A **piece** of something is less than the whole thing. Kelly gave Donna a **piece** of her apple. When the baseball hit the window, the glass broke into hundreds of **pieces**.

pig

A **pig** is an animal. **Pigs** are short and fat and have flat noses. They live on farms and are raised for their meat.

pig

pile

A **pile** is a lot of something all in one place. Some workers dug a hole for a new house. They left a big **pile** of dirt in the yard.

pilot

A **pilot** is a person who flies an airplane or a helicopter. You have to learn a lot to become a **pilot**.

pin

pin

A **pin** is a short, thin piece of metal with a sharp point. **Pins** are used to hold clothes together while they are being sewn.

pine

A **pine** is a kind of tree. **Pines** have needles on their branches. **Pine** needles stay green all winter.

pine

pink

Pink is a color. You can mix red paint and white paint to make **pink.**

pint

A **pint** is an amount of liquid. Two **pints** are the same as one quart.

pipe

pipe

A **pipe** is a tube made of metal, clay, or glass. **Pipes** are used to carry liquids from one place to another.

pirate

A **pirate** is someone who robs people on ships. Hundreds of years ago **pirates** sailed all over the world.

pizza

Pizza is a kind of food. It is flat and usually round. **Pizza** is baked with tomatoes, cheese, vegetables, or meat on top of bread.

place

A **place** is somewhere for something to be. Rooms, fields, and countries are all **places.** Even your cheek on your face is a **place.**

plan

1. A **plan** is an idea about how to do something. It is good to have a **plan** when you start to build something. **2.** To **plan** is to expect. We **planned** to go to the baseball game, but when it started raining we decided not to go. —**planned**

plane

Plane is another word for **airplane**. Bob's father knows how to fly a **plane**.

plant

plant

1. A **plant** is anything alive that is not a person or an animal. Most **plants** grow in the ground. Flowers, trees, and vegetables are all **plants**. **2.** To **plant** means to put seeds or small plants in the ground. The seeds Nina **planted** in the spring grew into big pumpkins by fall.

plastic

Plastic is something that things are made of. It can be thin or thick, soft or hard. **Plastic** can be any color.

play

1. To **play** is to have fun. Most people like to **play** games. You can **play** alone or with other people. **2.** To **play** is to make music with an instrument. Larry can **play** the trombone. **3.** A **play** is a kind of story. People act in **plays** while other people watch them. **Plays** are seen in theaters and on television.

player

A **player** is someone who plays. There are nine **players** on a baseball team.

playground

A **playground** is a place to play outside. **Playgrounds** usually have swings, seesaws, and other objects for people to play with. Most schools have **playgrounds**.

playground

please

Please is a word people use when they ask for something. Paco asked, "May I have an apple, **please**?"

plus

Plus means added. If you add two and three, you get five. Two **plus** three is five. Two **plus** three can also be written 2 + 3.

pocket

A **pocket** is a small bag of cloth. **Pockets** are sewn into jackets, coats, shirts, and pants. You can carry all kinds of things in your **pockets**.

pocket

poem

A **poem** is a group of words that are put together in a special way. People write **poems** to say things that are hard to say with usual language. The words in many **poems** rhyme.

poet

A **poet** is a person who writes poems.

point

1. A **point** is a sharp end. Pins, needles, and arrows have **points. 2.** To **point** is to show where something is. When Mark's brother asked where the moon was, Mark **pointed** to it in the sky with his finger.

point

pole

A **pole** is a long piece of wood or metal. Telephone **poles** hold wires up in the air.

police

The **police** are people whose job is to protect other people. But if people break the law, the **police** can put them in jail.

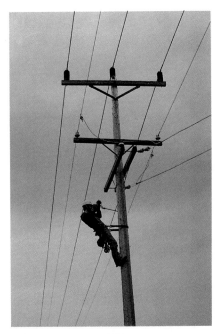

pole

235

pollution

Pollution is bad things in the air and water and in the ground. **Pollution** can make people, animals, and plants very sick.

pond

A **pond** is a large amount of water that is all in one place. Some **ponds** are big enough to swim in. A **pond** is smaller than a lake.

pony

pony

A **pony** is a kind of horse. **Ponies** are not as big as most horses. —**ponies**

poor

Poor is the opposite of rich. **Poor** people do not have much money.

popcorn

Popcorn is a kind of food. Pieces of **popcorn** get big and soft when they are cooked. They make a loud sound when they cook.

popcorn

possible

Possible means that something can happen. It is **possible** to teach some birds to talk. It is not **possible** to teach fish to write.

post office

A **post office** is a building. When you mail a letter, it goes to the **post office.** From there it goes to the person you are sending it to.

pot

A **pot** is a deep, round pan to cook food in. **Pots** are made of metal, glass, or clay. Most **pots** have handles.

potato

A **potato** is a vegetable. It has brown skin that is covered with bumps. **Potatoes** grow in the ground. —**potatoes**

potato

pound

A **pound** is an amount of weight. One **pound** is 16 ounces. Three apples weigh about one **pound.**

pour

To **pour** is to make liquid go from one place to another. Tina **poured** juice from a bottle into her glass.

powder

A **powder** is a lot of very tiny pieces of something. Flour is a kind of **powder.**

pour

power

1. Power is being able to do work. A bulldozer has enough **power** to move big piles of dirt. **2.** To have **power** means to be able to decide things. In the past, kings and queens had a lot of **power. 3. Power** means electricity. Our neighborhood had no **power** after the big storm.

practice

To **practice** is to do something many times so that you can do it well. People who play music have to take a lot of time to **practice.**

prepare

To **prepare** is to get ready. Bill **prepared** to go to camp by packing his clothes in a suitcase.

present¹

present¹

A **present** is a gift. People often give each other **presents** on their birthdays.

present²

The **present** is the part of time that is here now. This minute is part of the **present.**

pretend

To **pretend** is to make believe. When Jody acted in the school play, she **pretended** to be a princess.

pretty

Pretty means nice to look at. Everyone likes **pretty** flowers.

price

A **price** is how much money you have to pay for something. The **price** of a movie ticket is six dollars.

prince

A **prince** is the son of a king or a queen. The oldest **prince** may become king some day.

princess

A **princess** is the daughter of a king or a queen. Some **princesses** may become queens.

print

1. To **print** means to write with care so that none of the letters touch each other. George **printed** his name at the top of his paper. **2.** To **print** means to put letters on paper with a machine. Large machines are used to **print** books and newspapers.

prize

prize

A **prize** is something that you win. **Prizes** can be cups, ribbons, money, or many other things.

probably

Probably means that you are almost sure something is true. Steve comes to my house every Saturday. He will **probably** come this Saturday, too.

problem

A **problem** is something that causes trouble. Larry had a **problem** when he tore his pants in school.

promise

1. To **promise** is to say you will do something. When Les borrowed Josh's baseball glove, he **promised** to return it the next day. **2.** A **promise** is something that you say you will do. People should always keep their **promises.**

propeller

A **propeller** is a part of a machine. It is made of wood or metal. **Propellers** make planes and boats move by pushing against the air or water.

propeller

protect

To **protect** means to keep safe. An umbrella **protects** you from the rain or the sun.

proud

To be **proud** is to be glad to have people see what you have or what you have done. Sally was **proud** of the cake she made.

puddle

puddle

A **puddle** is a small amount of water that has collected in one place. Rain makes **puddles** in the street.

pull

To **pull** is to make something follow you. Charlie **pulled** a big box out of the garage and took everything out of it.

pumpkin

pumpkin

A **pumpkin** is a large fruit. **Pumpkin** pies are good to eat.

puppet

A **puppet** is a toy that looks like a small person or animal. Some **puppets** fit on your hand. Others are moved by strings from up above.

puppet

puppy

puppy

A **puppy** is a young dog. **Puppies** have soft fur and big feet. They like to play with everything. —**puppies**

purple

Purple is a color. Grape juice and grape jelly are usually **purple.**

push

To **push** is to make something go ahead of you. Lydia **pushed** her sister on the swing.

put

To **put** is to find a place for something and leave it there. Diane **put** a sandwich in her lunch box to take to school. —**put**

puzzle

1. A **puzzle** is a game. Some **puzzles** are pieces of paper or wood that you have to put together to make pictures. Other **puzzles** are hard questions that you work out in your head or with a pencil and paper. 2. A **puzzle** is also something that is hard to understand. It was a **puzzle** to Jane how her sister got home before she did.

A B C D E F G H I J K L M N O P Q R S T U V W X Y Z

a b c d e f g h i j k l m n o p q r s t u v w x y z

quart

A **quart** is an amount of liquid. There are four **quarts** in one gallon. A **quart** is a little smaller than a liter.

quarter

quarter

1. A **quarter** is a kind of coin. One **quarter** is the same as five nickels. Four **quarters** is the same as one dollar.
2. A **quarter** is one of four pieces that are the same size. You can cut a pie into **quarters**.

queen

A **queen** is a woman who rules a country. **Queens** usually rule for as long as they live. A **queen** can also be the wife of a king.

question

A **question** is a group of words that ask something that you want to know. Sometimes the teacher asks **questions** that nobody can answer.

quick

Quick means fast. The mouse was so **quick** that we almost did not see it.

quickly

Quickly means in a short time. Rob ate lunch **quickly** because he was late for the game.

quiet

To be **quiet** means to make very little sound. Our neighborhood is very **quiet** at night.

quite

1. **Quite** means all the way. David has three more pages to read. He has not **quite** finished the book.
2. **Quite** also means very. The weather can get **quite** hot here in the summer.

| A | B | C | D | E | F | G | H | I | J | K | L | M | N | O | P | Q | **R** | S | T | U | V | W | X | Y | Z |

| a | b | c | d | e | f | g | h | i | j | k | l | m | n | o | p | q | r | s | t | u | v | w | x | y | z |

rabbit

A **rabbit** is an animal. It has long ears and soft fur. **Rabbits** hop on their long back legs.

raccoon

A **raccoon** is an animal. It has short legs and dark marks like a mask over its eyes. **Raccoons** live in forests and fields.

rabbit

race

race

A **race** is a contest to find who is fastest. People have **races** on foot, in cars, on horses, and in many other ways.

radio

A **radio** is a machine that changes energy sent from other places into sound. You can hear music or news on the **radio.**

raft

raft

A **raft** is a kind of flat boat. Some **rafts** are made of logs. Others are made of boards.

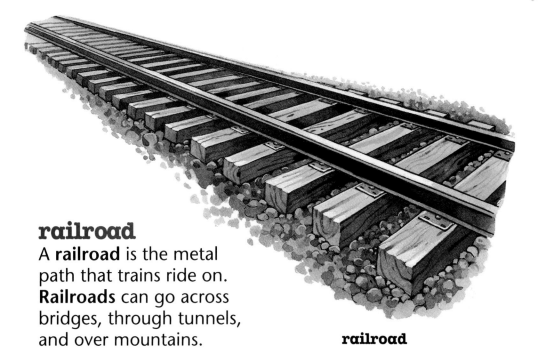

railroad

A **railroad** is the metal path that trains ride on. **Railroads** can go across bridges, through tunnels, and over mountains.

railroad

rain

1. Rain is water that falls in drops from clouds. Plants need **rain** to grow. **2.** To **rain** means to fall as drops of water. When it **rains,** everything gets wet.

rainbow

A **rainbow** looks like a ribbon of many colors across the sky. You can see a **rainbow** when the sun comes out after it rains.

raise

1. To **raise** is to lift up. Ella **raised** her hand to answer the question. **2.** To **raise** means to take care of something while it grows. Farmers **raise** vegetables. Parents **raise** children.

rainbow

rake

rake

1. A **rake** is a tool. It is made of long pieces of metal or wood joined together like fingers. The fingers are at one end of a long wood pole. **Rakes** are used to gather grass and leaves into piles. **2.** To **rake** is to gather into a pile with a rake. Paul helps his father **rake** the leaves in the fall.

ran

Ran is a form of **run.** Judy **ran** to school in the morning.

rang

Rang is a form of **ring.** The bell **rang** at the end of the day.

rat

A **rat** is an animal. It has a long tail, short fur, and sharp teeth. **Rats** are bigger than mice.

rat

reach

1. To **reach** means to put your hand out toward something. Ross **reached** in front of his sister for the bread. **2.** To **reach** also means to get all the way to. The big storm did not **reach** our part of the country.

read

To **read** means to look at words and know what they mean. Kay is learning to **read.** She often **reads** stories with her mother or father. —**read**

read

ready

When something is **ready,** people can use it. When the food is all cooked and hot, Mrs. Silva says, "Dinner is **ready!**"

real

Real means true. Maya likes to pretend, but Kathy likes stories about **real** people.

really

Really means that something is actually true. Pine needles do not look like other leaves. But they **really** are leaves.

reason

A **reason** is why something is so. Bad weather is the **reason** there was no school yesterday.

rectangle

A **rectangle** is a shape. **Rectangles** have four sides and four corners.

rectangle

red

Red is a color. Some apples and fire engines are **red.**

refrigerator

A **refrigerator** is a machine. Food and drinks are put inside **refrigerators** to keep them cold. Most people have **refrigerators** in their kitchens.

refrigerator

remember

To **remember** is to be able to find something in your mind. Laurie **remembers** the phone numbers of all her friends.

repeat

To **repeat** is to do or say again. I did not hear you. Would you please **repeat** what you said?

reptile

reptile

A **reptile** is a kind of animal. Snakes, turtles, and alligators are **reptiles.**

rest¹

To **rest** is to be still. People and animals need to **rest** when they are tired.

rest²

The **rest** of something is what is left. Lou ate half of his sandwich for lunch. He saved the **rest** for after school.

restaurant

A **restaurant** is a place where people go to eat meals. Most **restaurants** make many different kinds of food.

return

1. To **return** is to come back. Birds that have gone south in the winter **return** every spring. **2.** To **return** also means to bring back. Megan **returned** the books to the library after she read them.

rhinoceros

rhinoceros

A **rhinoceros** is a very large animal. It has short legs, gray skin, and one or two horns on its nose.

rhyme

To **rhyme** means to end with the same sound. *Cook* **rhymes** with *book. Group* **rhymes** with *soup. Tall* **rhymes** with *small.* Many poems use words that **rhyme.**

ribbon

A **ribbon** is a long, thin piece of cloth or paper. **Ribbons** come in many colors. Presents are often wrapped in paper and tied with a **ribbon.**

rice

Rice is a kind of food. Grains of **rice** are soft when they are cooked. **Rice** is the seeds of a kind of grass that grows in warm places.

rich

To be **rich** means to have a lot of money. **Rich** people often live in big houses and have fancy cars and other things.

ridden

Ridden is a form of **ride.** Tina likes to ride her bicycle. She has **ridden** it every day this week. Have you ever **ridden** on a horse?

riddle

A **riddle** is a kind of joke. It is a question that has a funny answer. "When does Thursday come before Wednesday?" is a **riddle.** The answer is "In a dictionary."

ribbon

rice

ride

1. To **ride** is to sit in or on something that moves. Cowboys **ride** horses. Children **ride** to school on a bus. **2.** A **ride** is a time when you ride in something. Every Sunday our family goes for a **ride** in the country. **3.** A **ride** is also a kind of machine at a fair. **Rides** turn people around or upside-down or carry them through the air. —**rode, ridden**

ride

right

1. **Right** means correct. Robin usually knows the **right** answer. **Right** is the opposite of wrong. **2.** **Right** also means the way something should be. The **right** way to get on a horse is from the side. **3.** **Right** is the opposite of left. In this country, people drive cars on the **right** side of the road.

ring¹

A **ring** is a circle that has an empty center. Some people wear **rings** of gold and silver on their fingers.

ring²

To **ring** is to make the sound of a bell. The school bell **rings** every morning when school starts. —**rang, rung**

ring¹

253

rise

To **rise** is to go up. The sun **rises** in the east every morning. The temperature outside **rises** on hot days. —rose, risen

risen

Risen is a form of **rise**. Mike wanted to watch the sun rise, but he slept too late. It had already **risen** when he woke up.

river

A **river** is a wide path of water that has land on both sides. Some **rivers** are hundreds of miles long.

river

road

A **road** is a wide path. **Roads** can go through fields, forests, and towns. People travel over **roads** in cars, trucks, and buses.

roast

To **roast** is to cook with hot air in an oven. Shari's mother **roasted** a big turkey for dinner on Sunday.

road

rob

To **rob** means to take something away from someone. Three people **robbed** the bank on Tuesday. They took all the money. —**robbed**

robin

A **robin** is a kind of bird.
Robins are red in front.

robot

A **robot** is a machine.
Robots are made to do
the same job over
and over.

rock

A **rock** is a hard object
in the ground. Some
rocks have metal in them.
Most of the earth is
made of **rock**.

rocket

A **rocket** is a machine.
It is a hollow tube
with something inside
that burns very fast.
Then the **rocket** flies
into the sky. Astronauts
are carried into space
on large **rockets**.

rode

Rode is a form of **ride**.
Len **rode** to school
on the bus this morning,
but he walked home.

roll

1. To **roll** is to keep turning over and over. When you
kick a ball, it **rolls** away. **2.** A **roll** is a kind of round
bread. People usually eat hamburgers in **rolls**.

robin

rocket

255

roller skate

A **roller skate** is a skate with wheels. **Roller skates** are not used on ice. They are for skating on floors or sidewalks.

roller skate

roof

A **roof** is the top of a building. Some **roofs** are flat. Others are shaped like triangles.

room

1. A **room** is an area in a building. **Rooms** usually have four walls, but they can be many different shapes or sizes.
2. **Room** means space. There is **room** for one more person on the couch with us.

roof

rooster

A **rooster** is a bird. Male chickens are **roosters**. **Roosters** make a lot of noise early in the morning.

root

A **root** is a part of a plant. It usually grows under the ground. Plants get food from the ground through their **roots**.

rooster

rope

Rope is made of several pieces of string twisted together. It can be thick or thin. **Rope** is tied in knots and used to hold things together. There are many kinds of **rope**.

rose¹

A **rose** is a kind of flower. **Roses** can be red, pink, yellow, or white. They grow on bushes and have a wonderful smell.

rose²

Rose is a form of **rise**. The sun **rose** this morning at six o'clock.

rough

Something that is **rough** does not feel even. The bark of most trees is **rough**. **Rough** is the opposite of smooth.

round

Round is a shape. A **round** object has no points or corners. Balls, wheels, and coins are **round**.

rope

rose¹

rub

To **rub** means to press something down and move it back and forth. Pat **rubbed** the window with a cloth to clean the dirt off. —**rubbed**

rubber

1. **Rubber** is something that is strong and easy to stretch. Tires for cars are made of **rubber.**
2. **Rubbers** are like shoes. They are made of rubber. People wear them over their shoes to keep their feet dry.

ruby

A **ruby** is a kind of jewel. **Rubies** are red. —**rubies**

rug

A **rug** is used to cover all or part of a floor. It is made of cloth or yarn. **Rugs** can be one color or many colors.

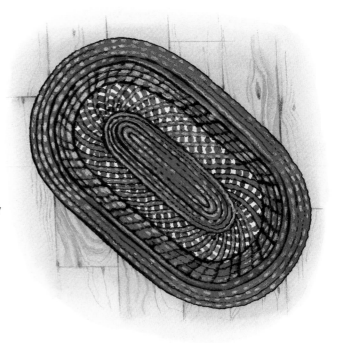

rug

rule

1. A **rule** tells how things or people must behave. To play a game right, you have to follow the **rules** of the game.
2. To **rule** is to make laws and decide things. Sometimes wars are fought over who will get to **rule** a country.

run

run

To **run** is to go somewhere by moving your legs quickly. Judy **ran** in a race with her friends.
—**ran, run**

rung

Rung is a form of **ring.** We know we are late for school because the bell has already **rung.**

rush

To **rush** means to hurry. Anne **rushed** home because she did not have much time to eat and get dressed for the party.

A B C D E F G H I J K L M N O P Q R S T U V W X Y Z

a b c d e f g h i j k l m n o p q r S t u v w x y z

sad

Sad means not happy. Jamie is **sad** because his best friend moved to another town. Everybody feels **sad** at some time. **—sadder, saddest**

safe

To be **safe** means to be in no danger. There was a terrible storm outside, but inside the house everyone was **safe.**

said

Said is a form of **say.** When Erica called her friend Michelle on the phone, the first thing Erica **said** was, "Hello!"

260

sail

1. A **sail** is a large piece of cloth on a boat. The **sail** catches the wind and uses it to make the boat move.
2. To **sail** is to make a boat or a ship move. Kay and Ruth **sailed** to a small island.

sail

sailor

A **sailor** is someone who sails a boat. **Sailors** know a lot about wind and water.

salt

Salt is something people put on food. It looks like white grains of sand. Ocean water has **salt** in it.

salt

same

To be the **same** means to agree in every way. **Same** is the opposite of different. Cathy and Laura both have blue eyes. Their eyes are the **same** color.

sand

Sand is made of tiny grains of rock. It covers beaches at the edge of lakes or oceans. **Sand** can feel rough or soft.

sand

261

sandwich

A **sandwich** is a kind of food. It is made of meat, cheese, peanut butter, or other things between two pieces of bread. Many people eat **sandwiches** for lunch.

sandwich

sang

Sang is a form of **sing**. Elizabeth learned a new song yesterday. She **sang** it all day long.

sat

Sat is a form of **sit**. Peter **sat** on the floor while he watched television.

Saturday

Saturday is a day of the week. **Saturday** comes after Friday and before Sunday.

saucer

A **saucer** is a small dish that isn't very deep. It usually fits under a cup. People sometimes put milk into **saucers** for cats to drink.

saucer

save

1. To **save** means to take out of danger. Firefighters often **save** the lives of people who are in danger.
2. To **save** also means to put away and keep. Lucy **saves** a little money every week. She has **saved** enough to buy a kite.

saw[1]

A **saw** is a tool. It is made of a flat piece of metal with a handle at one end. The edge of the metal piece has sharp points that are called teeth. **Saws** are used to cut wood, metal, and plastic.

saw[2]

Saw is a form of **see.** Erin looked out the window and **saw** two squirrels in the front yard.

saw[1]

say

To **say** means to speak words. When Brad answers the telephone, he **says,** "Hello!" **—said**

scare

To **scare** means to make afraid. A big dog **scared** Emily so much she ran all the way home.

scarecrow

A **scarecrow** is a pole covered with old clothes and a hat. **Scarecrows** are put in corn fields or other fields where vegetables are growing to scare away birds.

scarecrow

263

school

School is a place where students learn from teachers. Most children go to **school** from September until June.

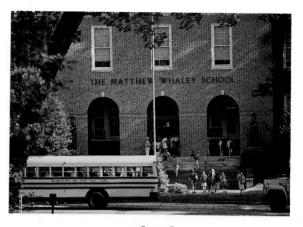

school

science

Science is what people know about the world and the things that are in it. The land, the ocean, the weather, the stars, medicine, plants, people, and animals are all parts of **science**.

scientist

A **scientist** is someone whose job is to learn about the world and the things in it. **Scientists** are curious about many things.

scientist

scissors

Scissors are a kind of tool. They are used to cut paper or cloth. Two pieces of metal are joined to make one pair of **scissors**. Each piece has one sharp edge and a hole for the fingers at one end.

scissors

scratch

To **scratch** means to make marks on something.
A rock can **scratch** a piece of glass. Cats can **scratch**
with their claws.

sea

Sea is another word for **ocean.** Many years ago
pirates sailed the **seas** looking for treasure.

seal

seal

A **seal** is a kind of animal. It has thick, smooth fur.
Seals swim in the ocean and eat fish.

season

A **season** is a part of
the year. There are four
seasons that come every
year. They are winter,
spring, summer, and
fall.

seat

A **seat** is anywhere you
can sit. Matt took a **seat**
in the back of the room.

seat

265

second¹

A **second** is a very short amount of time. Lightning flashes in about a **second**. There are 60 **seconds** in one minute.

second²

Second is next after first. The **second** letter of the alphabet is *B*.

secret

A **secret** is something nobody else knows. Becky told Chris where her hiding place was, but they didn't tell anybody else. They kept it a **secret**.

see

To **see** is to take things in with your eyes. Did you **see** the beautiful sunset yesterday? —**saw, seen**

seed

A **seed** is a part of a plant. New plants grow from **seeds**.

seed

seem

To **seem** means to look like. This **seems** like a good place to have a picnic.

seen

Seen is a form of **see**. Daniel likes to look at birds. He has **seen** about 100 different kinds of birds.

seesaw

seesaw

A **seesaw** is a kind of toy. It is a long board. People sit at opposite ends of the **seesaw,** and when one end goes up, the other end goes down.

sell

To **sell** means to give something for money. Donald **sells** glasses of juice outside his house on hot days. —**sold**

send

To **send** means to make someone or something go somewhere. Susan likes to **send** letters to her friends. Frank's mother **sent** him to the store to buy some bread.

sent

Sent is a form of **send.** Donna's grandfather **sent** her a present on her birthday.

sentence

A **sentence** is a group of words. Books are usually written in **sentences.**

September

September is a month of the year. It has 30 days. **September** comes after August and before October.

serious

Serious means not funny. When Bart is in a **serious** mood, he does not feel like laughing at jokes.

set

1. A **set** is a group of things that go together. Bud's mother has one **set** of blue dishes and one **set** of white ones. **2.** The sun **sets** when it goes below the edge of the sky. It was such a fine evening that everyone went out to watch the sun **set**.

seven

Seven is one more than six. **Seven** is written **7**. 6 + 1 = 7.

several

Several means more than three or four. Chris has **several** new books.

sew

To **sew** is to put pieces of cloth together with a needle and thread. Betsy **sewed** a dress for herself. —**sewn**

sew

sewn

Sewn is a form of **sew**. Ken has **sewn** two shirts for himself.

shadow

A **shadow** is a dark area with light around it. When there is a light behind you, you see your **shadow** in front. When the light is in front of you, your **shadow** is behind.

shake

1. To **shake** means to make something go up and down or from side to side very quickly. Sid **shakes** the jar to mix up the orange juice. **2.** To **shake** your head is to move your head from side to side. People **shake** their heads to say no.
—**shook, shaken**

shadow

shaken

Shaken is a form of **shake.** When our dog gets wet, we make sure he has **shaken** all the water off before he comes in the house.

shape

1. The **shape** of something is what it is like on the outside. Baseballs and basketballs have a round **shape.** Boxes have a square **shape. 2.** To **shape** is to give a shape to something. Dane's uncle **shaped** a piece of clay into a ball.

share

To **share** means to let everyone have some. Rick **shared** his birthday cake with everybody in his class.

shark

shark
A **shark** is a kind of large fish. **Sharks** have many sharp teeth and eat smaller fish.

sharp
To be **sharp** is to have a point or a thin edge that cuts. Some knives have **sharp** edges.

she
She means a female person. Mrs. Perez lives on our block. **She** is our neighbor.

sheep

sheep
A **sheep** is a kind of animal. It is covered with wool. **Sheep** are raised for their wool and their meat. —sheep

shell
A **shell** is hard skin on the outside of something. Eggs, lobsters, turtles, and nuts all have **shells**.

shell

shine

To **shine** is to send out a bright light. The sun **shines** every day when there are no clouds. —**shone**

ship

A **ship** is a big boat. It sails in deep water. Large **ships** can carry many people across the ocean.

shirt

shirt

A **shirt** is a kind of clothes. People wear **shirts** on the top part of their bodies. Many **shirts** have buttons.

shoe

A **shoe** is something that covers a foot. It may be made of leather, cloth, or plastic. People usually wear **shoes** over socks.

shoe

shoelace

A **shoelace** is a string that helps a shoe stay on your foot. Greg knows how to tie his **shoelaces**.

shone

Shone is a form of **shine**. The sun **shone** all day yesterday.

shoelace

271

shook

Shook is a form of **shake.** Sid **shook** the jar until the juice was all mixed up. When he asked Amy if she wanted any, she **shook** her head to say no.

shoot

1. To **shoot** is to go up or out quickly. Rockets **shoot** up into the air. **2.** To **shoot** also means to make go toward something. Ross **shoots** a basketball at the basket. —**shot**

shop

1. A **shop** is a small store. There are book **shops,** flower **shops,** hat **shops,** barber **shops,** and many other kinds of **shops. 2.** To **shop** is to go to a store to buy things. We **shop** at the supermarket for food. —**shopped**

shore

The **shore** is the land at the edge of the water. Oceans, lakes, ponds, and rivers all have **shores.**

short

1. Short is the opposite of tall. Ponies are **short** horses. **2. Short** is also the opposite of long. Tony had his hair cut **short. 3.** A **short** time is a small amount of time. It only took Jean and Kevin a **short** time to make their beds because they worked quickly.

short

272

shot¹

Shot is a form of **shoot**. Ross **shot** the ball into the basket.

shot²

A **shot** is a time when you shoot something. Ross made three **shots** before he hit the basket.

should

Should means that people want something to happen. Everyone **should** be in the room when class starts.

shoulder

A **shoulder** is a part of the body. It is between your neck and your arm.

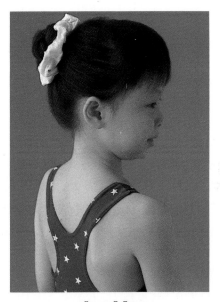

shoulder

shout

To **shout** is to talk in a loud voice. Ken **shouted** so that his friend could hear him across the street.

shovel

A **shovel** is a tool. It is made of a wide piece of metal joined to a long wood handle. **Shovels** are used to dig holes.

shovel

show

1. To **show** means to let someone see. Leslie **showed** Nina her books. **2.** To **show** also means to teach. Liz **showed** Edward how to skate. **3.** A **show** is a story that you see or hear on television or radio, at the movies, or in the theater. Many **shows** are on every week. —**shown**

shut

To **shut** means to close. Mary opened the door and came into the house. Then she **shut** the door behind her. —**shut**

shy

To be **shy** means to find it hard to talk to people. **Shy** people are often quiet. —**shier, shiest**

sick

To be **sick** is to have something wrong with you. Sometimes when you are **sick,** your head or your stomach hurts. Doctors and nurses take care of **sick** people.

side

A **side** is a flat part of the outside of something. A piece of paper has two **sides.** A square has four **sides.**

sidewalk

A **sidewalk** is a narrow path or road where people can walk. Usually there are **sidewalks** along the sides of streets.

sidewalk

sign

1. A **sign** is a symbol. The **signs** for plus and minus are + and −.
2. A **sign** is also a flat piece of metal or wood with a message printed on it. Road **signs** give people directions.

sign

silent

To be **silent** is to make no sound at all. Nick tried to stay **silent** so his sister would not find him hiding behind the door.

silly

To be **silly** means to act funny. Scott and his friends were giggling and running around the room. They were acting **silly**.

silver

Silver is a kind of metal. It is soft and white. **Silver** is used to make coins, jewelry, and other things.

silver

simple

Simple means not fancy. Helen can make a **simple** drawing of a person with only four lines and a circle.

since

Since means after. We have not had any rain **since** last month. The weather has been dry **since** then.

sing

To **sing** is to make music with your voice. Betty likes to **sing** songs as she walks. —**sang, sung**

sister

A **sister** is a girl who has the same parents as somebody else. Alec and his **sister** made supper for their parents.

sit

To **sit** is to rest your weight on something. Peter has his own chair to **sit** on at his desk. Last night he **sat** there to do his homework. —**sat**

sit

six

Six is one more than five. **Six** is written **6.** 5 + 1 = 6.

size

The **size** of something is how big it is. All tennis balls are the same **size**. People and clothes come in many different **sizes**.

skate

1. A **skate** is a kind of shoe. It has a long piece of metal or small wheels on the bottom. People wear **skates** to go fast on ice or on the sidewalk.
2. To **skate** is to go on skates. Anton can **skate** in a circle on one leg.

skate

ski

1. A **ski** is a long, narrow piece of wood, metal, or plastic. People wear **skis** on their feet to go fast on snow. **2.** To **ski** means to move over the snow on skis. Chris **skied** down a mountain.

ski

skin

The **skin** is the outside part of people, animals, and many plants. The **skin** protects what is inside.

skunk

skunk

A **skunk** is an animal. It is about as big as a cat. **Skunks** have big tails and white stripes on their backs. They can make a very strong smell to make other animals go away.

sky

The **sky** is the air far above the ground. It is blue during the day when there are no clouds. We see the sun, the moon, and the stars in the **sky. —skies**

sled

A **sled** is a toy. People ride on **sleds** over the snow. **Sleds** are made of wood, metal, or plastic.

sleep

Sleep is a time when your body is resting and not doing anything. Most people **sleep** in beds at night. This morning Angela **slept** until nine o'clock. —**slept**

sled

slept

Slept is a form of **sleep.** Jenny **slept** at her friend's house last night.

slow

To be **slow** means to take a long time. Turtles are very **slow.**

small

Small is the opposite of big. Todd's mother asked, "Would you like two **small** cookies or one big one?" Mice are **small** animals.

smell

1. To **smell** is to take in something through your nose. Craig **smelled** the smoke in the kitchen when the food burned in the oven. **2.** Something that **smells** is something you notice by smelling it. The bread baking in the kitchen **smells** wonderful. **3.** A **smell** is what something has that lets you smell it. Skunks can give off a very strong **smell.**

smile

1. A **smile** is a happy look on a person's face. The ends of the mouth turn up and the eyes wrinkle up.
2. To **smile** is to put a smile on your face. The clown **smiled** at the crowd.

smile

smoke

Smoke is made by things that burn. It looks like a cloud. **Smoke** can be white, gray, or black.

smooth

To be **smooth** is to feel even and have no rough spots. A piece of glass in a window is **smooth**.

snake

snake

A **snake** is a reptile. It has a long, narrow body and no arms or legs. Most **snakes** are small, but some can be very long.

sneaker

A **sneaker** is a kind of shoe. It has rubber on the bottom and cloth on the top. People wear **sneakers** when they run or play sports.

sneaker

sneeze

1. A **sneeze** happens when your nose itches. The air comes out of your nose and mouth very fast.
2. To **sneeze** is to make a sneeze. Some people **sneeze** three or four times before they stop.

snow

snow

1. Snow is tiny pieces of frozen water that fall from the clouds. In some places, **snow** covers the ground in winter. **2.** To **snow** means to fall as pieces of frozen water. When it **snows**, the ground becomes covered with snow.

so

1. So tells how much. Jamie thought of a joke. It was **so** funny that he could not stop laughing for an hour. **2. So** can mean also. Ann and Pat read the same book. Ann liked it, and **so** did Pat. **3. So** also tells why something happens. Chris forgot his umbrella, **so** he got wet when it rained.

soap

Soap helps take dirt off things when it is mixed with water. Rachel uses **soap** and water to wash her hands.

soccer

Soccer is a sport. In **soccer** two teams kick a ball up and down a field. They may not touch the ball with their hands.

soccer

sock

A **sock** is a kind of clothes. People wear **socks** on their feet, under their shoes.

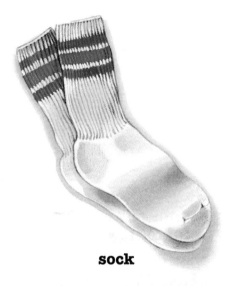

sock

soft

1. When something is **soft** it is easy to shape with your fingers and does not scratch. Fur and cotton are **soft**.
2. Soft is the opposite of loud. When Henry is in the library, he tries to be quiet. He speaks in a **soft** voice.

soil

Soil is the top part of the ground. Most plants grow in **soil**.

sold

Sold is a form of **sell**. Chico's father sells cars. Last week he **sold** four cars.

soil

solid

Solid means hard. Things made of wood and steel are **solid.**

some

1. Some means more than a few. Betty has not read most of the books in the library. But she has read **some** of them. **2. Some** also means an amount. The high mountains have **some** snow on them.

somebody

Somebody means any person. We do not know who won the race. But **somebody** must have won it.

someone

Someone is another word for **somebody. Someone** turned on the radio in my room while I was outside.

something

Something means any thing. The baby is hungry. She wants **something** to eat.

sometimes

Sometimes means at some times. **Sometimes** it rains during the winter and **sometimes** it snows.

somewhere

Somewhere means any place. That robin has a nest in the oak tree. Nobody can see the nest, but it is **somewhere** in the branches.

son

A **son** is someone's male child. Don's parents have two **sons.** One is Don and the other is Robert.

song

A **song** is what someone sings. Some **songs** are written for both instruments and voices together.

soon

Soon means in a short time. It is almost time for supper. We will be eating **soon.**

sorry

To be **sorry** is to feel sad about something. Kathy was **sorry** that Bob was sick. —**sorrier, sorriest**

sound

Sound is anything that you hear. Wind, thunder, dogs, and trains all make different **sounds.**

soup

soup

Soup is a kind of food. It is made with water and pieces of vegetables or meat. People eat **soup** from bowls.

sour

Sour is a kind of taste. Lemon juice tastes **sour.**

south

South is a direction. It is opposite north. If you look at where the sun rises, **south** is to your right.

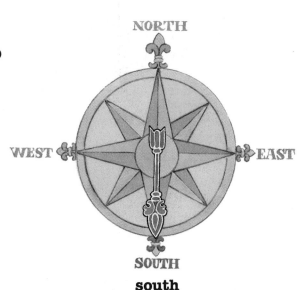

south

space

1. Space is a place where nothing is. Everything that you can see takes up **space**. There are **spaces** between the words on this page. **2. Space** is also everywhere outside our world. The sun, the moon, and the stars are in **space**.

speak

To **speak** is to say words. Sometimes Phil **speaks** in a soft voice. Other times he **speaks** loudly so that everyone can hear. —**spoke, spoken**

special

Special means important and not like all the rest. Holidays and birthdays are **special** days.

spell

To **spell** is to put letters together to make words. Nan knows how to **spell** most of the words in this book.

spell

spend

To **spend** means to give money to buy things. Jerry often **spends** his money on books. This morning he **spent** six dollars and bought three new books. —**spent**

spent

Spent is a form of **spend**. Kim **spent** most of her money on toys.

spider

A **spider** is a very small animal with eight legs. **Spiders** are not insects. But they catch insects in the webs they make.

spoke

Spoke is a form of **speak.** We could not hear the teacher in the back of the room, so he **spoke** louder.

spider

spoken

Spoken is a form of **speak.** Terry has **spoken** with a lot of people today.

spoon

spoon

A **spoon** is a tool to eat with. It looks like a tiny bowl with a handle. People eat soup and ice cream with **spoons.**

sport

A **sport** is a kind of game. Baseball, football, hockey, tennis, basketball, and soccer are all different **sports.**

spot

1. A **spot** is a small mark that is a different color from the area around it. Some animals are covered with **spots**.
2. A **spot** is also a place. Henry found a very nice **spot** to sit down.

spot

spring

Spring is a season. It comes after winter and before summer. The weather gets warmer and flowers begin to grow in the **spring**.

square

A **square** is a shape. All four sides of a **square** are the same length.

square

squirrel

A **squirrel** is a small animal. It has gray or red fur and a big tail. **Squirrels** live in trees.

stable

A **stable** is a building on a farm where horses and other animals are kept.

squirrel

stairs

Stairs are a group of steps. People walk up and down **stairs** to get from one floor of a building to another.

stamp

A **stamp** is a small piece of paper with words and numbers and a picture on it. People buy **stamps** to put on letters and packages they send through the mail.

stairs

stand

To **stand** is to keep your body straight and rest all your weight on your feet. Objects can **stand** on their legs or bases. Nate's desk **stands** by the door. —**stood**

stamp

star

1. A **star** looks like a tiny dot of light in the sky at night. There are millions and millions of **stars**, but they are very far away. Our sun is a **star**, too. **2.** A **star** is also a shape. It has five or six points. **3.** A **star** can also be an important person in movies, plays, or shows. **Stars** are people that almost everybody knows.

stare

To **stare** is to look long and hard at something. Rudy and Ted **stared** at a man who was wearing a funny hat.

start

1. To **start** is to do something when you have not been doing it before. I **started** to walk home at three o'clock. **2.** To **start** also means to begin going. The engine in a car **starts** when you turn the key.

station

A **station** is a special place or building. A train **station** is a place where trains stop. A gas **station** is where people buy gasoline for their cars. Television shows come from television **stations**. The police can be found at a police **station**.

station

statue

A **statue** is a kind of art. **Statues** usually look like people or animals. **Statues** are made from stone, clay, wood, or metal and can be small or large.

stay

To **stay** means to be in a place and not go away. Janet and Mickey **stayed** at school in the afternoon to play baseball with some other children.

statue

steady

Steady means not shaking. Judy held the ladder **steady** while Jake climbed up to the tree house.

steak

A **steak** is a kind of food. Most **steaks** are made of beef. They are cooked over a fire outside or in the oven.

steam

Steam is water that has become a gas. Water changes into **steam** when it boils. The **steam** goes into the air like thin smoke.

steam

steel

Steel is a metal. It is made from iron that has been melted. **Steel** is very hard and strong. It is used to make bridges, buildings, and many other things.

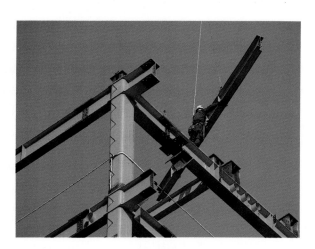

steel

step

1. A **step** is lifting one foot and putting it down. Tall people with long legs can take big **steps. 2.** A **step** is also a flat place where you can put your foot to go up or down. We walk up the **steps** to the front door of our house. **3.** To **step** is to move one foot in front of the other and walk. Eric **stepped** forward and raised his hand. —**stepped**

stick

stick

1. A **stick** is a piece of wood. Many **sticks** are old, dry branches of trees. Pat threw a **stick** for his dog to chase. **2.** To **stick** is to push into. Anne **sticks** her finger into the water to see how hot it is. **3.** To **stick** out means not to be in all the way. The branches **stick** out from the trunk of a tree. **4.** To **stick** together means not to come apart. Rick used glue to **stick** two pieces of paper together. —**stuck**

still

1. **Still** means that something has not stopped. My sister was mad at me yesterday. She is **still** mad at me today. **2.** **Still** also means not moving. When there is no wind, the water is very **still.**

stomach

The **stomach** is a part of the body. The food we eat goes into our **stomachs.**

stone

A **stone** is a small piece of rock. Smooth **stones** are found on the shores of oceans, lakes, and rivers.

stood

Stood is a form of **stand**. Stephanie's mother **stood** on a chair to reach some dishes.

stop

To **stop** means not to move. Buses **stop** at different places to let people get on and off. —**stopped**

store

A **store** is a place where things are sold. Shoes are sold in shoe **stores**. You can buy toys in a toy **store**. Some **stores** are very big and have all kinds of things to sell.

store

storm

A **storm** is a strong wind. **Storms** usually bring rain or snow. Many also have thunder and lightning.

story

A **story** is a group of words that tell what happened to people and places. **Stories** can be real or they can be made up. —**stories**

storm

stove

A **stove** is a metal box where people cook food. Food is cooked in pans on top of the **stove**.

straight

To be **straight** is to have no turns or curves. Bruce drew a **straight** line between two dots on his paper.

strange

Strange means different and hard to understand. New things often feel **strange** to us until we learn more about them.

stranger

A **stranger** is someone you do not know. Julie's family moved to a new town. They were **strangers** there until they met some new friends.

straw

A **straw** is a long tube made of paper or plastic. People can drink juice, water, or milk through **straws**.

stove

straw

stream

A **stream** is a narrow path of water. It moves in one direction. **Streams** are not as big as rivers.

street

A **street** is a road in a city or a town. Large cities have many **streets**.

street

stretch

To **stretch** is to change the shape of something by pulling it. Rubber and some kinds of plastic are easy to **stretch**.

string

String is used to tie things. It is made from long, strong plants or from a special kind of plastic. **String** comes in many different sizes and colors. Rope is made of many **strings** twisted together.

stretch

string bean

A **string bean** is a kind of vegetable. **String beans** are long and green. They grow on bushes.

string

strip

A **strip** is a narrow piece of something. Ribbons are made from **strips** of cloth or paper.

stripe

A **stripe** is a line of color. Zebras are covered with **stripes**. Len has a shirt with **stripes** on it.

stripe

strong

1. To be **strong** is to have a lot of power. Oliver is so **strong** that he can lift two full suitcases. **2. Strong** also means hard to break. Things made from steel are very **strong**.

stuck

Stuck is a form of **stick**. Jill **stuck** a pin into her finger by accident. Rick **stuck** two pieces of paper together with glue.

student

A **student** is someone who goes to school to learn. **Students** learn from teachers in class.

submarine

A **submarine** is a kind of ship that can travel underwater. **Submarines** are long and narrow.

submarine

subtract

To **subtract** is to take away one number from another number. When you **subtract** four from nine, you get five. The symbol for **subtract** is –. $9 - 4 = 5$.

subway

A **subway** is a train that travels through tunnels underground. **Subways** carry people through large cities.

such

Such means so much. Tom went to see his sister dance. He did not know she was **such** a good dancer.

sudden

To be **sudden** is to happen quickly without anyone expecting it. The **sudden** storm was a surprise to us.

suddenly

Suddenly means very quickly. We were having a good time at the picnic, when **suddenly** it began to rain.

suds

suds

Suds are many tiny bubbles made by soap and water. Chad likes to have a lot of **suds** when he washes the car.

sugar

Sugar is something people put on or in food. It is made of small white or brown grains that are sweet. Many desserts are made with **sugar**.

suit

A **suit** is a set of clothes that match. A jacket and pants or a jacket and a skirt made from the same cloth are a **suit**. Many men and women wear **suits** to work.

suitcase

A **suitcase** is a kind of box to carry clothes in when you travel. All **suitcases** have handles, and many have small wheels.

suit

summer

Summer is a season. It comes after spring and before fall. The weather is often hot during the **summer**. Many schools are closed in **summer**.

sun

The **sun** is a star. It is yellow. It shines in the sky during the day. The **sun** gives us heat and light.

suitcase

Sunday

Sunday is a day of the week. **Sunday** comes after Saturday and before Monday.

sung

Sung is a form of **sing.** Becky has been singing all morning. She has **sung** every song she knows three times.

sunlight

Sunlight is light from the sun. **Sunlight** is good for plants and animals.

sunny

A **sunny** day is a day when the sun is shining. People like **sunny** days when there is not a cloud in the sky.

sunrise

Sunrise is when the sun comes up. There is a **sunrise** every morning, but we can't see it if there are too many clouds.

sunset

Sunset is when the sun goes down. Many people like to go out to watch a beautiful **sunset.**

supermarket

A **supermarket** is a very big store where food is sold. You can get all kinds of food in a **supermarket.**

supermarket

supper

Supper is a meal. People eat **supper** in the evening.

suppose

To **suppose** means to think when you do not know for sure. When five students were late, we **supposed** it was because the school bus broke down.

sure

To be **sure** is to know. Addie was **sure** she had time to take the dog for a walk before dinner.

surface

surface

A **surface** is the outside or top part of something. Boats sail on the **surface** of the ocean. The **surface** of a mirror is smooth.

surprise

1. A **surprise** is something you did not expect. We thought today would be sunny. It was a **surprise** to us when it started to rain. **2.** To **surprise** someone is to do something they did not expect. Joe's friends **surprised** him with a party on his birthday.

swallow

To **swallow** is to make food go from your mouth to your stomach. Bart's mother tells him to chew his food before he **swallows** it.

swam

Swam is a form of **swim**. Peter **swam** all the way across the lake. Then he **swam** back.

swamp

A **swamp** is an area of land that is soft and wet. Frogs, mosquitoes, snakes, and alligators live in **swamps**.

swamp

swan

A **swan** is a large bird. It is usually white and has a long neck. People like to watch **swans** swimming on ponds and lakes.

swan

sweater

A **sweater** is a kind of clothes. People wear **sweaters** over their shirts. **Sweaters** are often made of wool or cotton.

sweet

Sweet is a kind of taste. Sugar, candy, cake, and cookies are **sweet**.

sweater

swim

To **swim** is to go
through the water
by moving your
arms and legs. Some
people can **swim**
long distances.
—**swam, swum**

swim

swing

1. To **swing** something is to move it from one side
to the other while holding it at one end. Tina **swings**
her bat to hit the ball. **2.** A **swing** is a seat held up by
ropes or chains. Children play on **swings** in parks or
playgrounds or in their yards. —**swung**

swum

Swum is a form of **swim.** Peter has been swimming
all morning. He must have **swum** about a mile.

swung

Swung is a form of **swing.** Ned **swung** his bat and
hit the ball.

symbol

A **symbol** is a mark
or a sign that means
something. Letters
of the alphabet
are **symbols**
for sounds. Words
are **symbols** for things.

syrup

syrup

Syrup is a thick, sweet
liquid. It is made from sugar
or the juice from some plants.

A B C D E F G H I J K L M N O P Q R S T U V W X Y Z

a b c d e f g h i j k l m n o p q r s t u v w x y z

table

A **table** is a kind of furniture. It has a flat top and legs. People sit at **tables** to eat.

tadpole

tadpole

A **tadpole** is a young frog. **Tadpoles** hatch from eggs. They are tiny and have tails. Some are black and some are clear.

tail

tail

A **tail** is a part of some animals' bodies. It can be long or short. An animal's **tail** is at the opposite end from its head.

take

1. To **take** means to bring toward you. Donna **takes** an apple out of the refrigerator and eats it. **2.** To **take** also means to bring with you. Kim **takes** books home from the library to read. **3.** To **take** can also mean to ride. Craig **takes** the bus to school in the morning. **4.** To **take** a picture means to use a camera to make a picture. Diane **took** three pictures of her brother. **5.** To **take** also means to be needed. It **takes** a lot of practice to play the piano well. —**took, taken**

taken

Taken is a form of **take.** When Diane had **taken** two pictures of her brother, he said "Please take one more!" Craig would have **taken** the bus this morning, but his father gave him a ride in the car instead.

talk

To **talk** is to speak with someone. Nicole and Pam **talked** about the picnic.

tall

To be **tall** is to stand high above the ground. Some trees grow very **tall**.

tame

To be **tame** is to do as people want. **Tame** animals make good pets. **Tame** is the opposite of wild.

tall

taste

1. To **taste** is to find out if something is sweet, sour, salty, or bitter. Sally put a berry in her mouth and **tasted** it. It **tasted** sweet. **2.** A **taste** is what something is like when you taste it. Lemons have a sour **taste**. Honey has a sweet **taste**.

taught

Taught is a form of **teach**. Katharine's parents **taught** her to read.

taxi

A **taxi** is a car that people pay to ride in. People take **taxis** to go from one place to another in the city.

taxi

teach

To **teach** is to show how to do something. Bob likes to **teach** his friends magic tricks. —**taught**

teacher

A **teacher** is a person who teaches other people. Most **teachers** work in schools.

team

A **team** is a group of people who work or play together. **Teams** can have different numbers of people. In many sports two **teams** play against each other.

team

tear¹

A **tear** is a drop of salt water. When people cry, **tears** come out of their eyes.

tear²

To **tear** is to pull something into two pieces. Lenny likes the sound it makes when he **tears** a piece of paper in half. —**tore, torn**

teddy bear

A **teddy bear** is a kind of toy. It is soft and brown. **Teddy bears** can be large or small.

teeth

Teeth means more than one **tooth**. People chew food with their **teeth**.

teeth

telephone

A **telephone** is an object that sends voices from one place to another. **Telephones** use electricity to send voices over wires.

telescope

A **telescope** is a tool that helps people see things that are far away. **Telescopes** are made of curved pieces of glass or mirrors inside a tube. People can use them to look at the stars.

television

Television is an object that makes pictures and sounds. A television station uses electricity to send the pictures and sounds through the air to the **television**.

tell

1. To **tell** is to talk about something. After Bob does a magic trick, he **tells** his friends how he did it. **2.** To **tell** also means to know. Susan can **tell** that winter is coming because the days are getting shorter. —**told**

telephone

telescope

television

temperature

The **temperature** of something is how hot or cold it is. The inside of an oven has a high **temperature**. Ice and snow have low **temperatures**.

ten

Ten is one more than nine. **Ten** is written **10**. 9 + 1 = **10**.

tennis

Tennis is a sport. In **tennis**, two or four people hit a ball back and forth across a wide net.

tennis

tent

A **tent** is a place to sleep when you camp. **Tents** are large pieces of cloth held up with poles and ropes.

terrible

Terrible means very bad. Many trees were broken in the **terrible** storm.

test

A **test** is a way to find out what someone can do. Teachers often give **tests** in school. There are many kinds of **tests**.

than

Than tells how much. Dennis likes summer weather more **than** he likes winter weather.

thank

To **thank** means to tell someone you are glad they did something for you or gave something to you. Alice **thanked** her friends for the birthday presents they gave her.

that

1. **That** means something not near you. I can see two cars on the street. One car is near me. This car is blue. The other car is far away. **That** car is red.
2. **That** is used to put two parts of a sentence together. Ellen told her mother **that** she wanted a new dress.

the

The tells which one. Joan does not want just any dog. She wants to keep **the** dog that followed her home from school.

theater

theater

A **theater** is a building where people watch movies or plays. Some **theaters** are very large.

their

Their means belonging to them. Elena reads her book. Kate reads hers. They both read **their** books.

theirs

Theirs means belonging to them. The students all bought some fish for an aquarium. The fish are **theirs.**

them

Them means more than one. There are some birds in Nancy's yard. She feeds **them** seeds and bread.

themselves

Themselves means them and nobody else. Babies have to be dressed because they cannot dress **themselves.**

thermometer

A **thermometer** is a tool that is used to measure temperature. Some **thermometers** show how hot or cold it is outside. Others are used to show the temperatures of people who are sick.

thermometer

then

1. **Then** means at that time. It is cold now. But it was not cold last summer. The weather was warm **then.**
2. **Then** also means next. Paul pulled his sled up the hill. **Then** he rode back down again.

there

1. **There** means at that place. "Where should I put these logs?" Gail asked her father. He pointed to the fireplace. "Put them down **there,**" he said. 2. **There** is or **there** are mean that something can be found. "**There** is a chicken in the back yard!" Steve shouted.

these

These means more than one of **this.** If you will carry those books, I'll carry **these.**

they

They means more than one. Sarah and Penny ran on the beach. Then **they** ran into the water.

they're

They're is a short way to say **they are.** Bret and Alec are not here yet. **They're** coming in ten minutes.

thick

thick

1. Thick means big and heavy. Felix found a board so **thick** he could not hit a nail through it. **Thick** is the opposite of thin. **2.** To be **thick** also means to be hard to pour. Honey is **thick.**

thin

thin

Thin means having the front and back close together. A piece of paper is **thin. Thin** is the opposite of thick. **Thin** is also the opposite of fat.

thing

1. A **thing** is an object, animal, or plant. You can see many interesting **things** in a museum. **2.** A **thing** can also be what someone does. Patty gave Carol some of her lunch. That was a nice **thing** for her to do.

think

1. To **think** means to use your mind. Sam **thinks** about what he will do on Saturday. **2.** To **think** also means to believe. Ellen's brother **thinks** the moon is made of cheese. Ellen **thought** so too until she saw it through a telescope. —**thought**

third

Third is next after second. The **third** letter of the alphabet is C.

thirsty

To be **thirsty** is to need to drink. When you are **thirsty,** your mouth gets dry.

this

This means something that is near you. Sean likes the hat he has on. "**This** is my favorite hat," he says.

those

Those means more than one of **that.** I have read these books on the table but not **those** on the chair.

thought

1. **Thought** is a form of **think.** When the teacher asked a question, Ray **thought** about his answer before he spoke. **2.** A **thought** is also something a person thinks about. Maggie had many happy **thoughts** about her trip last fall.

thousand

A **thousand** is a number. **Thousand** is written **1,000**. There are ten hundreds in a **thousand**. **Thousands** of people went to watch the football game.

thread

Thread is very thin string. It comes in many different colors. People sew clothes with a needle and **thread**.

thread

three

Three is one more than two. **Three** is written **3**. 2 + 1 = **3**.

threw

Threw is a form of **throw**. Tad **threw** a tennis ball against the barn until his arm got tired.

through

Through means from one side to the other. Jess walked **through** a field to get to school. A bird flew into our house **through** an open window.

throw

throw

To **throw** is to make something go through the air. Troy **throws** the ball and Scott catches it.
—**threw, thrown**

thumb

A **thumb** is a part of the hand. **Thumbs** are like short, strong fingers. People have one **thumb** on each hand.

thunder

Thunder is a loud noise in the air. It is made when lightning flashes.

thumb

Thursday

Thursday is a day of the week. **Thursday** comes after Wednesday and before Friday.

ticket

A **ticket** is a small piece of paper. When Janet and Amy went to the theater, they bought two **tickets** so they could go in to see the movie.

tie

1. To **tie** is to hold something together with string or rope. George keeps his boat **tied** to the dock.
2. To **tie** also means to make knots in string or rope or ribbon. Joy **ties** pretty bows on all the presents. **3.** A **tie** is a kind of clothes. It is a narrow piece of cloth that people wear around their necks. **Ties** come in many different colors.

tie

tiger

A **tiger** is a large wild animal. It looks like a very big cat. **Tigers** have fur with black stripes.

tiger

tight

To be **tight** means to be hard to take off or apart. Dick's shoes felt **tight** because they were too small for him. **Tight** is the opposite of loose.

time

1. **Time** is how long it takes for something to happen. The past, the present, and the future are all parts of **time.** Cathy lives close to school. It only takes a short **time** for her to walk there. If she has **time,** she always stops at her friend Susanna's house on the way.
2. **Time** is also the hour on the clock when something happens. "What **time** does the movie start?" "It starts at eight o'clock." 3. A **time** is how often something is done. The band played a song once. Then they played it again. They played the song two **times.**

tin

Tin is a kind of metal. It is used to make cans, toys, and other things.

tiny

Tiny means very, very small. Ants and flies are **tiny** insects. Grains of sand are the **tiniest** things we can see. —**tinier, tiniest**

tire

A **tire** is a circle of rubber. It covers the outside of a wheel. Cars have four wheels and four **tires.**

tire

tired

To be **tired** is to feel weak and need rest. Karen has played basketball all afternoon. Now she is **tired.**

to

1. To tells where something goes. Astronauts have flown **to** the moon. **2. To** also means until. The store opens at nine o'clock. It closes at six o'clock. It is open from nine **to** six. **3. To** also tells how something changes. Michael painted the yellow walls white. He changed the walls from yellow **to** white.

today

Today means this day. Yesterday came before **today.** Tomorrow comes after **today.**

toe

A **toe** is a part of the foot. People have five **toes** on each foot.

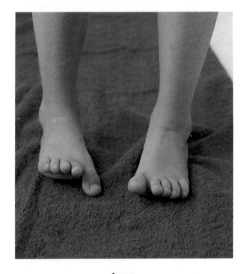

toe

together

Together means with each other. Nina and Maria walked to school **together.**

told

Told is a form of **tell.** Ellie **told** us about her trip yesterday.

tomato

A **tomato** is a fruit. It is round and red. Ketchup is made from **tomatoes.** —**tomatoes**

tomorrow

Tomorrow is the day after today. **Tomorrow** is in the future. If today is Monday, then **tomorrow** will be Tuesday.

tomato

tongue

The **tongue** is a part of the body. It is in your mouth. People use their **tongues** to help them eat and speak.

tonight

Tonight is the night between today and tomorrow. Megan does her homework this afternoon so she can watch television **tonight.**

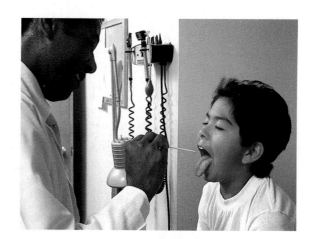

tongue

too

1. **Too** means also. Allison can play two instruments. She plays the violin, and she plays the piano **too.**
2. **Too** also means more than what is good. It is **too** hot to work outside today.

took

Took is a form of **take.** Al **took** his books off the table. Barbara and Cindy **took** the bus to school. Beth **took** pictures of her family with her new camera. It **took** the artist many months to make that statue.

tool

A **tool** is something people use to help them work. Hammers, rakes, spoons, knives, and shovels are all **tools.**

tool

tooth

A **tooth** is a part of the body. It is in your mouth. **Teeth** are hard and white. People chew food with their **teeth. —teeth**

toothbrush

toothbrush

A **toothbrush** is a small brush with a handle. People use **toothbrushes** to clean their teeth after meals.

top

The **top** is the highest part of something. Joanna had to stand on her toes on a chair to reach the **top** of the refrigerator. **Top** is the opposite of bottom.

tore

Tore is a form of **tear**[1].
Jill **tore** her jacket
on a fence on the way
home from school.

tornado

A **tornado** is a very
strong wind. It is
shaped like a cone
that twists in the air.
Tornadoes can
knock down houses
and pull trees out of the
ground. —**tornadoes**

tornado

touch

To **touch** is to feel something with your body. Carrie
burned her finger when she **touched** the hot oven.

toward

Toward means in the
direction of. The ship
seemed to grow bigger
as it sailed **toward** us.

towel

A **towel** is a rectangle
of cloth. **Towels** are used
to take water off things.
People use **towels** to dry
themselves after they
take a bath or go swimming.

towel

town

A **town** is a place where people live and work. Most
towns are smaller than cities.

toy

A **toy** is an object that people play with. Wood blocks, dolls, and kites are **toys.**

toy

tractor

A **tractor** is a machine. It has big wheels and a strong engine. Farmers use **tractors** to help prepare the ground to plant vegetables in.

traffic

Traffic means cars, trucks, and buses on city streets. At some times of the day there is a lot of **traffic.**

tractor

trail

A **trail** is a path through a field or a forest. People and animals can make **trails.**

trailer

A **trailer** is like a large box on wheels. **Trailers** can be pulled by tractors and trucks to carry things. Some people use **trailers** as houses or offices.

trailer

train

A **train** is a group of railroad cars. **Trains** carry heavy loads from one place to another.

train

trap

1. A **trap** is a way to catch wild animals. Some **traps** are made of steel. Other **traps** are holes in the ground. **2.** To **trap** is to catch an animal or a person in a trap. Spiders **trap** insects in their webs. —**trapped**

trash

Trash is something people do not want. Loren puts the **trash** out beside the street every Thursday.

trash

travel

To **travel** means to go and visit another place. Every year Leslie's family likes to **travel** to some place they have never seen before.

treasure

Treasure is a pile of gold, silver, and jewels. Hundreds of years ago pirates gathered **treasures** from all over the world.

tree

A **tree** is a kind of plant. It has branches and leaves. **Trees** can grow to be very tall. Wood comes from **trees**.

triangle

A **triangle** is a shape. **Triangles** have three straight sides. Steve drew lines between three dots to make a **triangle**.

trick

1. A **trick** is something that seems impossible. Kurt saw a magician make a rabbit disappear. He knew it was a **trick** because nobody can make something really disappear.
2. To **trick** is to get someone to do something he or she does not want to do. When Chris's dog was sick, it did not want to take its medicine. Chris's mother **tricked** the dog by putting the medicine in its food.

tree

triangle

trip

1. A **trip** is a time when you travel somewhere. Our family took a **trip** to the mountains last year.
2. To **trip** means to hit something with your foot and fall down. Kelly **tripped** on a rock as she was climbing the hill. —**tripped**

trombone

A **trombone** is an instrument. It is a kind of horn. **Trombones** are made of long metal tubes that fit together.

troop

A **troop** is a group of people. Many **troops** of boys and girls went to camp last summer.

trouble

1. Trouble is something that makes it hard to know what to do. Nick does not add or subtract very well. He has **trouble** with numbers. **2.** To be in **trouble** means that someone is angry with you. Lenny tore his new shirt playing football. He knew he would be in **trouble** when he got home.

trousers

Trousers are a kind of clothes. People wear **trousers** over their legs. Most **trousers** have pockets in them.

trombone

trousers

truck

A **truck** is a machine. It is like a very large car that is used to carry heavy loads. Stuart's brother has a job driving a **truck**.

truck

true

To be **true** is to match the way things are in the world. It is **true** that the world is round. It is not **true** that snow is purple.

trumpet

A **trumpet** is an instrument. It is a kind of horn. **Trumpets** are made of metal tubes. The sound of a **trumpet** can be very loud.

trumpet

trunk

1. A **trunk** is the thick middle part of a tree. The **trunk** of a tree grows up from the ground. Branches grow out of it. **2.** A **trunk** is also part of an elephant. It is like a very long nose. Elephants can pick up things with their **trunks**. **3.** A **trunk** can also be a large box. People often pack clothes and other things in **trunks** when they travel.

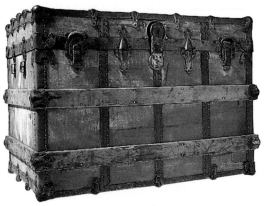

trunk

trust

To **trust** someone is to believe they will do as they say. Betsy and Bonnie are best friends. They **trust** each other not to tell their secrets to anyone else.

truth

The **truth** is what is true. If people do not tell the **truth**, you cannot trust them.

try

1. To **try** is to work to make something happen. Cheryl **tries** to run faster than her sister, but she is too little.
2. To **try** means to do or taste something you never have before. Lou has **tried** new flavors of ice cream, but he still likes vanilla the best. —**tries, tried**

tub

A **tub** is a wide, round, open kind of bucket. **Tubs** are made of wood, metal, or plastic. They are used to store things in or to take baths in.

tube

A **tube** is a long, hollow piece of metal, glass, rubber, or plastic. Most **tubes** are used to carry liquids or gases from one place to another.

tube

Tuesday

Tuesday is a day of the week. **Tuesday** comes after Monday and before Wednesday.

tug

To **tug** is to pull hard at something. Small children sometimes **tug** at their parents' coats to get their attention.
—**tugged**

tugboat

A **tugboat** is a boat with a very strong engine. **Tugboats** push and pull large ships when there is not much room for them to move.

tulip

A **tulip** is a kind of flower. It is shaped like a cup. **Tulips** come in several colors.

tulip

tunnel

tunnel

A **tunnel** is a long hole under the ground. Some **tunnels** go through mountains so that people can travel from one place to another.

turkey

1. A **turkey** is a kind of bird. It has a long neck. **Turkeys** are raised for their meat. Some **turkeys** are wild. **2. Turkey** is a kind of meat. It comes from a turkey.

turkey

turn

1. To **turn** is to move in a circle. The wheels on a bicycle **turn** when the bicycle moves. **2.** To **turn** your head is to move it from side to side. Craig **turned** his head to see who had come into the room. **3.** To **turn** a page is to move it so you can see the other side. **4.** To take **turns** means that one goes, and then the other. Barbara and Meg shared a sandwich. First Barbara took a bite of it, then Meg did. They took **turns** until the sandwich was gone.

turtle

A **turtle** is a reptile. It can live both in the water and on the land. A **turtle** can pull its head, legs, and tail inside its shell.

turtle

twice

Twice means two times. Anita liked the movie so much she saw it **twice**.

twin

twin

A **twin** is one of two children born at the same time to the same parents. Most **twins** look alike.

twist

To **twist** is to turn around and around. Rope is made of pieces of string that are **twisted** together.

two

Two is one more than one. It is the second number when you count. **Two** is written **2**. $1 + 1 = 2$.

ABCDEFGHIJKLMNOPQRST**U**VWXYZ
abcdefghijklmnopqrst**u**vwxyz

ugly
Ugly means not nice to look at. We found some old **ugly** coats in the attic.

umbrella
An **umbrella** is something you use to protect yourself from rain or sun. It is shaped like an upside-down bowl with a long handle. The top part is made of cloth and metal.

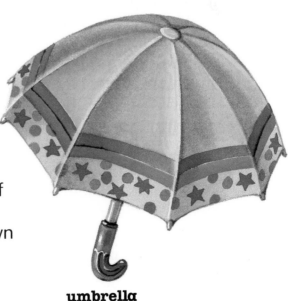

umbrella

uncle

An **uncle** is the brother of your mother or father. An **uncle** can also be your aunt's husband. Fritz has six **uncles**.

under

1. Under means lower than the bottom of something. Water flows **under** a bridge. **2. Under** also means lower than the surface of something. The roots of a plant grow **under** the ground.

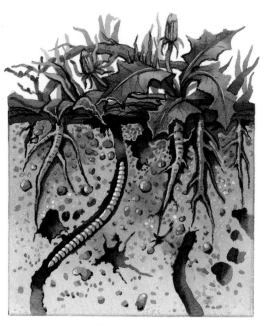

underground

underground

Underground means under the ground. Worms live **underground**.

underline

To **underline** is to draw a line under something. Leon **underlines** his name on the page. People often **underline** things that are important.

understand

To **understand** something means to know it well. Jackie knows how to read. She **understands** all the words on this page.
—**understood**

underline

understood

Understood is a form of **understand**. I did not understand how to play the game. Then Pete explained the rules to me and I **understood** it.

underwater

underwater

Underwater means below the surface of the water. Nancy and George know how to swim **underwater**. One day they explored an **underwater** cave.

uneasy

Uneasy means not feeling safe. Lily was a little bit afraid to go on an airplane for the first time. She was **uneasy** about it.

uneven

Uneven means not smooth or straight. It was hard for us to walk in the field. The ground was very **uneven** there.

unhappy

Unhappy means sad. Mitch was very **unhappy** when his best friend moved away.

unicorn

A **unicorn** is an animal in stories. It is not real. A **unicorn** looks like a horse with one long horn on its head.

uniform

A **uniform** is a special kind of clothes. People wear **uniforms** to show that they belong to a group. Police, nurses, and sports teams wear **uniforms**.

unicorn

universe

The **universe** is everything in our world and in space put together. The earth, the sun, the moon, and the stars are all part of the **universe**.

unlucky

Unlucky means having bad luck. Bess wanted to have a picnic last Saturday, but it rained. She wanted to have a party on her birthday, but she got sick. Bess is very **unlucky**.

uniform

untie

To **untie** something means to take the knots out of it. Mike **untied** his shoelaces by himself.

until

Until means up to that time. Alan is in school every day from nine o'clock **until** three o'clock.

unusual

Unusual means not usual. It would be **unusual** to have snow in the summer.

up

up

1. **Up** means going from a low to a high place. We went **up** in a balloon. 2. **Up** also means at or in a high place. My books are **up** in the closet.

upon

Upon means on. The bird was sitting **upon** the branch.

upset

To be **upset** is to feel angry, hurt, or unhappy. Vanessa was **upset** when her best friend did not come to her party.

331

upside-down

Upside-down means with the top side down and the bottom side up. Leo knocked his dessert off the table by accident. It landed **upside-down** on the floor.

us

Us is a form of **we.** My brother and I walked to the store. At the store we met our aunt. She gave **us** a ride home in her car.

upside-down

use

To **use** means to do work with something. A carpenter **uses** tools, wood, and nails to build a house.

useful

Something is **useful** if it helps you do something. Tools are **useful** for fixing and building things.

usual

Something **usual** is something that you can expect to happen. It is **usual** for it to be hot in the summer.

usually

Usually means almost always. Tina **usually** rides her bicycle home from school.

A B C D E F G H I J K L M N O P Q R S T U V W X Y Z

a b c d e f g h i j k l m n o p q r s t u V w x y z

vacation

A **vacation** is a time when people do not work or go to school. This year our whole family is going on **vacation** to the mountains.

valley

A **valley** is an area of land between hills or mountains. **Valleys** often have rivers that go through them.

valley

vanilla

Vanilla is a flavor. It is made from a kind of seed. **Vanilla** is used in ice cream and other desserts.

vanilla

vegetable

vegetable

A **vegetable** is a plant or a part of a plant that you can eat. Lettuce, onions, and peas are **vegetables.**

very

Very means more than what is usual. Bears are big animals. Elephants are **very** big animals.

village

A **village** is a small group of houses. It is usually in the country. **Villages** are not as big as towns.

village

violin

A **violin** is an instrument. It has four strings. A kind of thin stick is pulled across the strings to make music.

visit

To **visit** is to stay somewhere or with somebody for a time. Our class **visited** the zoo last week. Ted and Laura **visit** their grandmother every Sunday.

voice

A **voice** is the sound people make when they talk or sing or shout. I heard a **voice** in the other room.

violin

vowel

A **vowel** is a kind of letter. A, E, I, O, and U are **vowels. Vowels** and consonants make the letters of the alphabet.

Ww

ABCDEFGHIJKLMNOPQRSTUV**W**XYZ

abcdefghijklmnopqrstuv**w**xyz

wagon

A **wagon** is used
to carry people
or things from one
place to another.
It has four wheels.
Large **wagons** are
sometimes pulled
by horses.

wagon

wait

To **wait** means to stay someplace until something
happens. Eric **waited** ten minutes on the sidewalk
for the bus to come.

wake

To **wake** up means to become awake. Tracy usually **wakes** up early in the morning, but today she **woke** up late. —**woke, woken**

walk

1. To **walk** means to move by taking steps. Mara **walks** to school every day. **2.** A **walk** is when you go somewhere by walking, especially for fun. Henry likes to go for **walks** on the beach.

walk

wall

1. A **wall** is a side of a room. Most rooms have a ceiling, a floor, and four **walls**. **2.** A **wall** is something that is built to keep one place apart from another. The farmer built a stone **wall** around his field.

wall

want

To **want** something means that you would like to have it. Peter **wants** a trumpet more than anything.

war

A **war** is a time when people or armies fight against each other. Many people die in **wars**.

warm

Warm means not very hot. When it is cold outside, our dog likes to stay in the house where it is **warm.**

was

Was is a form of **be.** Yesterday I **was** late to school. Today I will be early.

wash

To **wash** something means to clean it with soap and water. On Thursdays it is Benjamin's turn to **wash** the dishes.

wash

wasn't

Wasn't is a short way to say **was not.** Alec went to Mario's house to see him, but he **wasn't** there.

watch

1. To **watch** means to look at something to see what it will do. Cindy **watched** her father while he fixed her bicycle. **2.** A **watch** is a small clock you wear on your wrist. Carl looked at his **watch** to see what time it was.

watch

water

Water is a kind of liquid. It is clear and it has no taste. People, plants, and animals need **water** to live.

wave

1. To **wave** means to move your hand from side to side. Jason **waves** hello when he sees his cousins. **2.** A **wave** looks like a long bump that moves through the water in a lake or an ocean. Our boat went up and down on the **waves**.

wave

wax

Wax is used to make candles and crayons. It melts easily when it is heated. Bees make one kind of **wax**. Other **waxes** are made from plants or oil.

way

1. A **way** is how you get from one place to another. We took the long **way** home. **2.** A **way** also means how something is done. Alice was acting in a funny **way**.

wax

we

We is a word you use when you speak about yourself and somebody else together. My brother and I are going to the library. **We** want to borrow some books.

weak

1. Weak is the opposite of strong. I am too **weak** to lift that heavy box. **2. Weak** means easy to break. There are many cracks in that wall. It looks very **weak.**

wear

To **wear** something means to have it on your body to cover or protect you. When it is cold outside, Jane **wears** a coat, a hat, boots, and gloves.
—**wore, worn**

weather

Weather is what it is like outside. When the **weather** is warm, Bud likes to go to the lake. In cold **weather** he likes to ski.

web

A **web** is a group of threads that a spider makes. Spiders make **webs** to catch insects to eat.

web

Wednesday

Wednesday is a day of the week. **Wednesday** comes after Tuesday and before Thursday.

week

A **week** is an amount of time. There are seven days in one **week.** There are 52 **weeks** in one year.

weigh

To **weigh** means to measure how heavy something is. Many kinds of food are **weighed** before you buy them.

weight

Weight is how heavy something is. The doctor weighs James to see how much he has grown. She tells him his **weight** every time he visits her.

weigh

welcome

To be **welcome** means that someone is glad to see you or to do something for you. We tried to make our new neighbors feel **welcome.** "Thank you for the beautiful gift," Dara said to Anita. "You're **welcome,**" Anita said.

well¹

A **well** is a deep hole in the ground. Most **wells** are dug to get water, oil, or gas.

well¹

well²

1. Well means in a good way. Alison plays the violin **well.** Everyone likes to listen to her. **2. Well** means healthy. Ed stayed home because he was sick. When he is **well** he will go to school again.

we'll

We'll is a short way to say **we will. We'll** bring something to eat to the party.

went

Went is a form of **go.** Sometimes Rob and Randy go places together. Last Saturday they **went** bowling.

were

Were is a form of **be.** Lee and Kris will be home today. They **were** away on vacation all last week.

we're

We're is a short way to say **we are.** My sisters and I are very good at sports. **We're** also good at painting and drawing.

weren't

Weren't is a short way to say **were not.** Jim and Mark **weren't** hungry after they ate their supper.

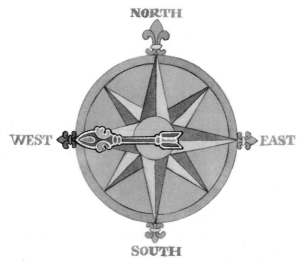

west

west

West is a direction. The sun sets in the **west. West** is the opposite of east.

wet

Wet means covered with water or full of water. Emily got **wet** when she walked in the rain.

wet

we've

We've is a short way to say **we have. We've** lived in our house for two years.

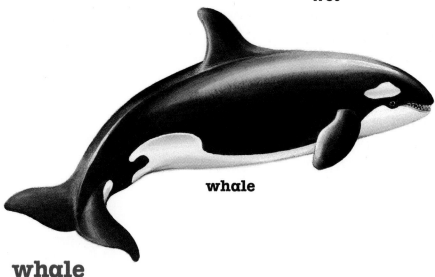
whale

whale

A **whale** is a large animal that lives in the ocean. Some **whales** are the biggest kind of animal in the world.

what

What is used to ask questions about people and things. **What** are you having for dinner? **What** book are you reading?

whatever

Whatever means anything or everything. Pablo eats **whatever** his father cooks for him.

wheat

Wheat is a kind of plant. The seeds of **wheat** are made into flour. **Wheat** is an important food.

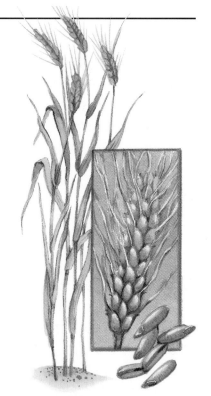

wheat

wheel

A **wheel** is a round object. **Wheels** turn to help machines move or work. A car has four **wheels**.

when

1. **When** is used to ask questions about time. **When** does the basketball game start? 2. **When** means at what time. All the snow melts **when** the weather gets warm.

where

1. **Where** is used to ask questions about a place. **Where** are we? 2. **Where** means at what place. Sue found the key on the table **where** her brother had left it.

wheel

which

Which is used to ask questions about one person or thing in a group. **Which** of these coats is yours? **Which** girl is your friend?

while

1. While means during what time. Amy went to the store **while** it was open. **2.** A **while** is a small amount of time. We played for a **while.**

whisper

To **whisper** means to speak in a soft voice. People **whisper** in a library so they won't bother other people.

whistle

1. To **whistle** means to make a musical sound by blowing air through your teeth or lips. Many people learn to **whistle** songs. **2.** A **whistle** is a kind of toy. It is a very small instrument that you blow into. **Whistles** make a noise like a bird.

whistle

white

White is a color. It is a very light color. This page is printed on **white** paper.

who

1. Who is used to ask questions about a person. **Who** knocked on the door? **2. Who** tells which person. The man **who** works in the store is very friendly.

whoever

Whoever means any person. **Whoever** runs the fastest will win the race. My parents said I could invite **whoever** I wanted to my party.

whole

Whole means all together. Our **whole** class went to the museum.

whom

Whom is a form of **who**. Who did Dan see in the park? Anne is the girl **whom** he saw.

who's

1. **Who's** is a short way to say **who is**. **Who's** in the kitchen? 2. **Who's** is also a short way to say **who has**. **Who's** been to the zoo?

whose

Whose tells who something belongs to. The teacher found a glove that someone had lost. She wanted to know **whose** glove she had found.

why

Why is a word people use when they ask about or explain what makes things happen. **Why** do birds fly south for the winter? Annie doesn't know **why** she likes ice cream. She just does.

wide

1. **Wide** means having a lot of space between the two sides. Jim's desk was too **wide** to fit through the door. 2. **Wide** tells how far something is from side to side. The island is three miles **wide**.

width

Width is how wide something is. The **width** of Darleen's paper is eight inches.

wife

A **wife** is a married woman. She is the **wife** of the man she married. —**wives**

wild

wild

Wild means not grown or cared for by people. The movie was about **wild** animals.

will

Will tells about something in the future. Gail **will** go to the beach with Elena tomorrow. —**would**

win

To **win** means to finish first or to do the best in a game or a race. When people play a game, someone **wins** and someone loses. —**won**

win

wind

Wind is air that moves. Strong **winds** blew the tree down.

windmill

A **windmill** is a machine. The power of the wind makes it work. Some **windmills** bring up water from the ground. Some help make electricity.

windmill

window

A **window** is an open place in a wall. It lets light and air into a room. **Windows** usually have glass in them.

wing

A **wing** is a part that helps something to fly. All birds have **wings**. Bats and many insects also have them. Most airplanes have two **wings**.

wing

winter

Winter is a season. It comes after autumn and before spring. **Winters** can be very cold in some places.

wire

A **wire** is a piece of metal in the shape of a long string or thread that is easy to bend. Electricity moves through **wires**.

wire

348

wish

1. A **wish** is something that you hope will happen. Rachel made a **wish** when she blew out the candles on her birthday cake. **2.** To **wish** for something means to hope that it will happen. Mel **wishes** that he could find a hidden treasure.

witch

A **witch** is a woman who has magic powers. We read about good and bad **witches** in stories.

with

1. With means together. I went to the store **with** my sister. Joe's hamburger came **with** onions on it.
2. With tells what something has. A giraffe is an animal **with** a long neck. **3. With** can also tell what you use to do something. Brian dug a hole **with** a shovel.

without

1. Without means not having. People cannot live **without** air and food. **2. Without** means not with someone or something else. Casey walks to school alone. She goes **without** anyone else.

wives

Wives means more than one **wife**. **Wives** and husbands are married to each other.

wizard

A **wizard** is a magician. The **wizard** in the movie had long white hair and a pointed hat.

woke

Woke is a form of **wake**. Terry **woke** up and got dressed for school.

woken

Woken is a form of **wake**. It is nine o'clock, but Bob has not **woken** up yet.

wolf

A **wolf** is a wild animal. It looks like a large dog. **Wolves** hunt for food in groups. —**wolves**

wolf

wolves

Wolves means more than one **wolf**. **Wolves** have thick fur.

woman

A **woman** is a grown female person. A girl grows up to be a **woman**. —**women**

women

Women means more than one **woman**. Girls grow up to be **women**.

won

Won is a form of **win**. My sister's soccer team **won** most of their games this year.

wonder

To **wonder** means to think about something that you are curious about. I **wonder** what I will be when I grow up.

wonderful

Wonderful means very good. Gary liked the book he just finished. He thought it was **wonderful**.

won't

Won't is a short way to say **will not.** Rose **won't** be seven years old until next spring.

wood

1. Wood is what trees are made of. It is used to make houses, furniture, and paper. **2.** The **woods** is a place where a lot of trees grow. We went for a walk in the **woods.**

wood

wool

Wool is the hair that grows on sheep. **Wool** is used to make yarn and cloth for clothes and blankets. Many sweaters are made of **wool.**

word

A **word** is a sound or a group of sounds that means something. People speak or write **words** to share their thoughts with other people.

wool

wore

Wore is a form of **wear.** Everybody in the play **wore** a funny costume.

work

1. Work is the energy you use to do or to make something. Digging a hole is hard **work. 2. Work** is also what someone does for a job. Ted's sister is a scientist. She loves her **work. 3.** To **work** means to do work. Claudia is writing a book. She **works** on it every day. **4.** To **work** also means to act right. That radio is broken. It doesn't **work** now.

worker

A **worker** is a person who works. Kerry works in an office. She works hard at her job. She is a good **worker.**

world

The **world** is the place where everyone lives. All the land and the oceans make up our **world.**

worm

A **worm** is a small animal. It has a long soft body and no legs. Many **worms** live in the ground.

worm

worn

Worn is a form of **wear.** Jerry's jacket is new. He has not **worn** it before today.

worry

To **worry** means to feel that something bad may happen. My parents **worry** sometimes if I am late coming home. **—worries, worried**

worse

Worse means very bad, but not as bad as the worst. Yesterday it rained. Today the weather was **worse.** It rained and snowed. **Worse** is the opposite of better.

worst

Worst means worse than any other. Dave did not like the soup his sister made at all. He thought it was the **worst** thing he had ever tasted. **Worst** is the opposite of best.

would

Would is a form of **will.** Carl said yesterday that he **would** go swimming with us today.

wouldn't

Wouldn't is a short way to say **would not.** The cat **wouldn't** come down from the tree.

wrap

To **wrap** means to cover something, as with paper or cloth. People usually **wrap** birthday presents and tie them with bows. Michael **wrapped** the puppy in a blanket. —**wrapped**

wrap

wrinkle

A **wrinkle** is a crooked line or bump on something when it is folded up. When John frowns he gets **wrinkles** on his face. Lisa used an iron to get the **wrinkles** out of her shirt.

wrinkle

wrist

A **wrist** is a part of the body. It is between your hand and your arm. You wave your hand by bending your **wrist**.

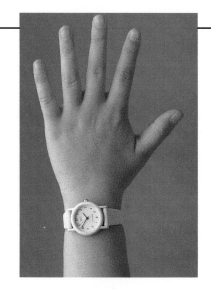

wrist

write

1. To **write** means to make letters and words on a piece of paper with a pencil or a pen. Diane **wrote** her name in big letters across the page.
2. To **write** means to make up a story, a poem, a play, or music. Authors **write** stories and poems for other people to read and enjoy.
—**wrote, written**

written

Written is a form of **write**. Lesley has **written** many letters to his friend Emilio.

write

wrong

Wrong means not correct. Margo gave the **wrong** answer to the teacher's question. The teacher told her the right answer.

wrote

Wrote is a form of **write**. Morgan **wrote** the date at the top of the page.

ABCDEFGHIJKLMNOPQRSTUVW**X**YZ

abcdefghijklmnopqrstuvw**x**yz

x-ray

An **x-ray** is a kind of energy. It can pass through objects. Doctors use **x-rays** to take pictures of the inside of the body.

xylophone

A **xylophone** is an instrument. It is made of a row of wood rectangles. The rectangles are different sizes. They make different notes when they are hit with small hammers.

xylophone

355

Y y

ABCDEFGHIJKLMNOPQRSTUVW**X**Y**Z**

abcdefghijklmnopqrstuvw**x**y**z**

yard¹

yard¹

A **yard** is an amount of length. One **yard** is the same as three feet. A **yard** is almost as long as a meter.

yard²

A **yard** is an area of land around a house. Many **yards** are covered with grass.

yard²

356

yarn

Yarn is a kind of string. It is made from wool, cotton, or other threads that are twisted together. **Yarn** is used to make sweaters and socks.

yarn

yawn

To **yawn** is to open your mouth wide and take a deep breath. People **yawn** when they are tired.

year

A **year** is an amount of time. There are 12 months in one **year.**

yell

To **yell** means to shout. The hockey game was very exciting. We **yelled** for our team.

yawn

yellow

Yellow is a color. Bananas are **yellow.**

yes

Yes means that you agree. Beth asked Susan to come to her house after school. Susan said, "**Yes,** I would like to come."

yesterday

Yesterday is the day before today. It snowed **yesterday.** Today the ground is covered with snow.

yet

Yet means up to this time. The movie has not started **yet**.

you

You is a word that is used when one person speaks to another person. I like **you. You** look tired today. Do **you** like to dance?

you'll

You'll is a short way to say **you will.** Let's play this new game. I think **you'll** like it.

young

young

To be **young** means to have been alive only a short time. Children are **young** people. **Young** is the opposite of old.

your

Your means belonging to you. That is **your** house.

you're

You're is a short way to say **you are. You're** tall for your age.

yours

Yours means belonging to you. That cup is **yours.**
This one is mine.

yourself

Yourself means you and nobody else. Did you earn
that money **yourself?**

you've

You've is a short way to say **you have. You've** got
a nice smile.

yo-yo

A **yo-yo** is a kind of
toy. It is made of
a piece of string
tied between two
round pieces. The
yo-yo goes up and
down on the string.
Some people can do
tricks with **yo-yos.**

yo-yo

A B C D E F G H I J K L M N O P Q R S T U V W X Y **Z**

a b c d e f g h i j k l m n o p q r s t u v w x y z

zebra

zebra

A **zebra** is an animal. It looks like a small horse. **Zebras** have black and white stripes.

zero

Zero is a number. It is written **0**. 1 + **0** = 1.
One hundred is written with a one and two **zeroes.**
—**zeroes**

zipper

zipper

A **zipper** is used to hold parts of clothes together.
It is made of plastic or metal. It has two rows of little
bumps that look like teeth. These rows fit together
when the **zipper** is closed up.

zoo

A **zoo** is a place where animals are kept. Many
of them are kept in cages. You can see lions, tigers,
and elephants at some **zoos.**

PHONICS AND SPELLING

A Guide to Spelling

Here are examples of different ways for spelling vowel and consonant sounds.

Short Vowel Sounds

◆ Short a

Short **a** (as in **at**) is often spelled a :

act	cap
bad	glass
bag	fast
began	flash

Short **a** may be spelled au :

laugh

cap

◆ Short e

Short **e** (as in **pet**) is often spelled e :

best	hen	spend
desk	insect	step
egg	leg	tell
fed	mess	them
fresh	neck	wet

Short **e** is sometimes spelled ea :

bread	instead	measure
dead	lead[1]	read
feather	leather	treasure
head	meant	weather

363

Short **e** may also be spelled with these letters:

a	any, many	u	bury
ai	said	ue	guess
ie	friend		

ring

◆ Short i

Short **i** (as in **pit**) is often spelled i :

big	fit	ring
bin	ink	sick
disease	lid	sister
disk	lip	wish
fist	miss	with

Short **i** is sometimes spelled y :

gym
symbol

Short **i** may also be spelled with these letters:

e	pretty	u	busy
			business
o	women		
		ui	build
			building

◆ Short o

Short **o** (as in **hot**) is often spelled o :

body	monster
copy	pop
costume	rock
knot	solid

costume

Short **o** may be spelled a :

> watch

◆ Short u

Short **u** (as in **nut**) is often spelled u :

brush
bucket
bus
butter
fun
hug
hunt
luck

bucket

lump
much
mud
must
puppy
rung
summer
tub

Short **u** may also be spelled o :

color   love   some
done   month   son
from   mother   tongue
honey   nothing

In some words, short **u** is spelled ou :

double   touch
rough   trouble

double

Short **u** may also be spelled
with these letters:

 a   was

 oe   does

 oo   blood, flood

365

Long Vowel Sounds

◆ Long a

Long **a** (as in **ate**) is often spelled [a] or [a-consonant-e] :

able	radio	strange
made	rake	take
male	safe	tape
page	same	wave

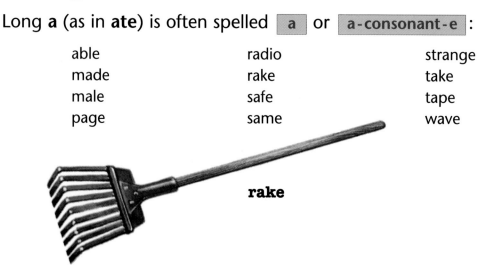

rake

Long **a** may also be spelled with these letters:

[ai]		[ea]	
	aid		break
	daisy		great
	grain		steak
	paid		
	pail	[ei]	eight
	painter		neighbor
	raise		weigh
	wait		weight

[ay]		[ey]	
	hay		they
	played		
	maybe		

hay

◆ Long e

Long **e** (as in **see**) is often spelled [e] or [e-consonant-e] :

be	me
evil	she
he	these

Long **e** may also be spelled ee :

bee
cheese
deep
feel
feet

freeze
seed
teeth
tree
week

bee

Long **e** may also be spelled ea :

bead
clean
east
heap
leaf

leave
please
seat
speak
teacher

Long **e** may also be spelled with these letters:

 ie   believe
piece

 i   piano
ski

 y   baby
family
hurry
pretty
many

 eo   people

◆ Long i

Long **i** (as in **ice**) is often spelled
 i or i-consonant-e :

describe
dime
find
fire
hide
I
iron

like
mine
nice
pint
size
smile
write

smile

367

Long **i** may also be spelled [y] or [y] with another letter:

[y]	by	[ey]	eye
	fly		
	my	[ye]	dye, good-bye
	rhyme		
	xylophone	[uy]	buy

Long **i** is sometimes spelled [i] plus one or more silent consonants:

[igh]   flight, sigh

[is]   island

xylophone

◆ Long o

Long **o** (as in **go**) is often spelled [o] or [o-consonant-e] :

both	joke	robe
fold	lone	rode
home	note	so
hope	owe	those

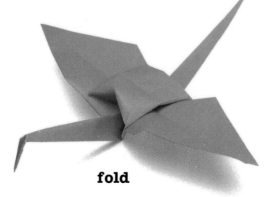

fold

Long **o** may be spelled oa :

coat	loaves
loaf	road
loan	soap

Long **o** may also be spelled ow :

below	show
grow	throw
know	yellow

loaf

Long **o** may be spelled oe :

toe

◆ Long u

Long **u** (as in **use**) is often spelled u or u-consonant-e :

computer	music
cute	uniform

Long **u** may also be spelled in these ways:

 ew   few

 eau   beautiful

Other Vowel Sounds

The sound of **a** in **all** may be spelled with these letters:

al	talk	aw	awful	au	caught
	walk		crawl		saucer
			jaw		taught
all	call		paw		
	fall		saw	ough	fought
	small		straw		thought
	tall		yawn		ought

369

The vowel sound in **how** may be spelled in these ways:

ow			ou	
clown			about	
cow			house	
flower			our	
now			proud	
powder			round	
towel				

round

The vowel sound in **good** may be spelled in these ways:

oo		u	
book		bull	
hood		full	
look		put	
took		pull	
wood			

The vowel sound in **moon** may be spelled in these ways:

oo	u	oe
cool	June	canoe
food	ruby	shoe
loose	supermarket	
soon	truth	ui
rooster		fruit
smooth	ou	suit
too	group	
tooth	soup	
troop	through	
	you	

o	ew
lose	blew
move	flew
to	grew
who	
whose	ue
	blue
	glue
	true

shoes

The vowel sound in **joy** may be spelled in these ways:

oy	cowboy	oi	boil
	toy		noise
			oil

toy

Consonant Sounds

Some consonant sounds have more than one spelling. Here are some to remember:

The sound of **f** as in **fun** may be spelled in these ways:

f	after	ff	different	gh	enough
	fall		off		laugh
	if				rough
	life	ph	phone		
	perfect				

The sound of **j** as in **jam** may be spelled in these ways:

j	injure	g	energy	dg	edge
	jelly		ginger		judge
	jog		imagine		
	jump		magic		
	object		page		

The sound of **ch** as in **much** may be spelled in these ways:

ch	bunch	tch	catch
	chalk		scratch
	child		stretch
	choose		watch
	rich		
	touch	ti	question

The sound of **k** as in **kick** may be spelled in these ways:

k		**c**		**ck**	
	keep		because		back
	park		car		hockey
	sky		helicopter		rocks
	speak		macaroni		
	woken		picnic	**ch**	Christmas
	wrinkle		uncle		school

The sound of **r** as in **red** may be spelled in these ways:

r, rr				**rh**	
	border		our		rhinoceros
	borrow		ran		rhyme
	far		spring		
	green		story	**wr**	wrap
	hurry		tree		wrist
	more		work		write

The sound of **s** as in **say** may be spelled in these ways:

s, ss		**c**		**sc**	
	base		cent		muscle
	disappear		city		science
	fast		dance		scissors
	loose		December		
	miss		nice	**st**	castle
	pants		pencil		listen
	sit		princess		whistle

The sound of **sh** as in **ship** may be spelled in these ways:

sh		**ci**	
	push		magician
	shut		special
	wash		
		s	sugar
ti	dictionary		sure
	direction		
	pollution	**ch**	machine

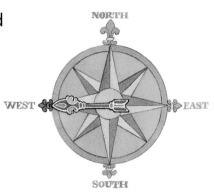

direction

Compound Words

Many long words are made up of two short words joined together. These are called **compound words**. Here are some examples from this Dictionary.

afternoon
basketball
bathtub
birthday
cannot
cowboy
drugstore
earthquake
firefighter
fisherman
flashlight
goldfish

grasshopper
grownup
haircut
homework
horseshoe
jellyfish
lighthouse
newspaper
nobody

outside
pancake
playground
popcorn
railroad
rainbow
scarecrow
shoelace
sidewalk
something
toothbrush
tugboat

goldfish

The compound words in the list below are made up of short words given in this Dictionary. Can you tell what they mean?

back + pack = backpack
class + room = classroom
corn + bread = cornbread
dish + towel = dishtowel
door + bell = doorbell
farm + land = farmland
grape + vine = grapevine

hair + brush = hairbrush
moon + light = moonlight
mouse + trap = mousetrap
paint + brush = paintbrush
pine + cone = pinecone
rain + drop = raindrop
sail + boat = sailboat

Words That Sound Alike

Many words sound alike but have different spellings and meanings. For example, two things that match each other are a **pair**, as in "a pair of boots." There is also a kind of fruit that is called a **pear**. The words **pair** and **pear** are spelled differently and have different meanings, but they sound alike when you say them out loud.

sounds like

pair   **pear**

Here are some examples of words that sound alike in this Dictionary.

ate	eight	knight	night	son	sun
bare	bear	knot	not	their	there
be	bee	know	no	threw	through
blew	blue	lead[1]	led	to	too, two
cent	sent	mail	male	wait	weight
dear	deer	meat	meet	way	weigh
eye	I	one	won	weak	week
flour	flower	pair	pear	wear	where
for	four	peace	piece	which	witch
heal	heel	right	write	who's	whose
hear	here	road	rode	wood	would
hole	whole	sea	see	your	you're
knew	new	sew	so		

Special Names for Words

Words have special names that tell how they are used.

A **noun** is a word that names a person, a place, or a thing. In these examples, the nouns are underlined.

- ◆ The <u>dog</u> dug a <u>hole</u> in the <u>yard</u>.
- ◆ My <u>father</u> wrote a <u>book</u> about <u>horses</u>.
- ◆ <u>Baseball</u> is my favorite <u>sport</u>.

A **pronoun** is a word that can take the place of a noun. It names the same person, place, or thing as the noun it stands for. The words **I, you, he, she, it, we,** and **they** are pronouns. In each of these examples, the noun and the pronoun that takes its place are underlined.

- ◆ <u>Anna</u> read the book. <u>She</u> enjoyed the story.
- ◆ Bees make <u>honey</u>. <u>It</u> is very sweet.

honey

A **verb** is a word that names an action. In these examples the verbs are underlined.

- ◆ The cat <u>jumped</u> over the fence and <u>ran</u> away.
- ◆ Bob <u>caught</u> the ball and <u>threw</u> it to Lisa.

An **adjective** is a word that tells about a person, a place, or a thing. In these examples, the adjectives are underlined.

- ◆ The <u>little</u> child began to cry.
- ◆ The library was very <u>quiet</u>.
- ◆ A nickel is equal to <u>five</u> cents.

nickel

Spelling Strategies

1 Naming more than one

Most words add **s** to name more than one.

books	hills	peas
cats	jobs	puddles
cows	judges	rings
days	lambs	thanks
hamsters	months	tops
hands	notes	turkeys

Words that end in **s, x, sh,** or **ch** add **es** to name more than one.

boxes
buses
dishes
messes
watches

dishes

Words that end in **consonant-y** change the **y** to **i** and add **es** to name more than one.

cherry	cherries	jelly	jellies
city	cities	party	parties
daisy	daisies	story	stories

Some words have special spellings to name more than one.

child	children	mouse	mice
foot	feet	tooth	teeth
man	men	woman	women

2   Adding *ed* or *ing*

The final **e** in some words is dropped before adding **ed** or **ing**.

breathe	breathed, breathing
care	cared, caring
hope	hoped, hoping
move	moved, moving

The final consonant in some words is doubled before adding **ed** or **ing**.

fit	fitted, fitting
hop	hopped, hopping
hug	hugged, hugging
rub	rubbed, rubbing

3   Contractions

A **contraction** is a short form of a word or a group of words.
An **apostrophe** (') takes the place of the missing letter or letters.

can't	=	cannot	they're	=	they are
don't	=	do not	we've	=	we have
I'm	=	I am	you'll	=	you will

4   Proper names

A **proper name** is the name of one particular person, place, or thing. Proper names begin with a capital letter.

Names of people	George Washington
Names of places	North America
Names of months	September
Names of the days of the week	Sunday
Names of holidays	Thanksgiving Day
Names of languages	English

377

Picture Credits

Commissioned Photographs

Albano Ballerini add, address, against, alphabet, apart, bag, between, boot, bowl, breakfast, cereal, cup, dinner, dish, doll, doughnut, empty, equal, fold, fork, full, hammer, honey, iron, kettle, lock, lunch, magnet, meal, nickel, pair, pancake, patch, pen, pencil, penny, popcorn, quarter, refrigerator, saucer, shoe, shoelace, silver, skates, soup, spoon, stamp, steam, suitcase, syrup, thermometer, thread, toothbrush, trunk, wheel, yard

Phoebe Ferguson alike, alone, awake, away, backward, bed, behind, book, both, cap, carry, copy, costume, cut, desk, draw, drop, ear, earn, expand, eye, face, fancy, feet, fill, finger, fist, flat, front, frown, gift, heavy, heel, help, hide, ill, ink, ladder[1], lead[1], letter, loose, make, measure, mess, mix, pack, palm, pocket, pour, puppet, sew, shadow, shoulder, stretch, sweater, teeth, thumb, tie, toe, towel, trombone, trumpet, twin, underline, violin, whistle, wrap, wrist, write, xylophone

Photography

above Magnus Rietz, The Image Bank; **airplane** Ted Russell, The Image Bank; **aquarium** E.R. Degginger, Animals, Animals; **arm** John P. Kelly, The Image Bank; **art** Dave Forbert, SuperStock; **artist** SuperStock; **asleep** Bob Daemmrich, Stock, Boston; **astronaut** © 2003 PhotoDisc, Inc./Getty Images; **automobile** Ron Anderson, Midwestock; **baby** Dag Sundberg, The Image Bank; **balloon** Joe Azzara, The Image Bank; **band** Luis Castaneda, The Image Bank; **barber** © 2003 PhotoDisc, Inc./Getty Images; **barn** Donald Specker, Animals, Animals; **baseball** Paul Barton, The Stock Market; **basketball** Kirk Schlea, Picture Perfect, USA; **beach** © 2003 PhotoDisc, Inc./Getty Images; **bear** Johnny Johnson, Animals, Animals; **bend** Kim Robbie, The Stock Market; **beside** Ariel Skelley, The Stock Market; **bicycle** Kaz Mori, The Image Bank; **bird** Robert Lankinen, The Wildlife Collection; **blacksmith** Southern Living, Photo Researchers, Inc.; **board** Bruce Roberts, Photo Researchers, Inc.; **boat** Gary L. Benson, Allstock; **bone** John Cancalosi, Peter Arnold, Inc.; **bowling** Blair Seitz, Photo Researchers, Inc.; **branch** Luis Castaneda, The Image Bank; **bread** Alfredo Tessi, The Image Bank; **bridge** Greg Probst, Allstock; **bubble** Craig Hammell, The Stock Market; **bull** Joe Azzara, The Image Bank; **bulldozer** Frank Siteman, Stock, Boston; **bus** Larry Kolvoord, The Image Works; **camel** Tomas D.W. Friedmann, Allstock; **can²** © 2003 PhotoDisc, Inc./Getty Images; **canoe** Renee Lynn, Photo Researchers, Inc.; **car** Amanda Clement, The Image Bank; **castle** Blaine Harrington III, The Stock Market; **cat** Sebastiao Barbosa, The Image Bank; **cattle** Chuck Kuhn, The Image Bank; **cave** Pedro Coll, The Stock Market; **cheek** Bob Daemmrich, Stock, Boston; **chicken** Gabe Palmer, The Stock Market; **chimney** E. Faure, SuperStock; **circus** Chuck Place, The Image Bank; **climb** Bruce Forster, Allstock; **clown** Renzo Mancini, The Image Bank; **computer** © 2003 PhotoDisc, Inc./Getty Images; **cook** SuperStock; **cow** Don Mason, The Stock Market; **cowboy/cowgirl** Don King, The Image Bank; **crooked** Thomas Ives, The Stock Market; **crowd** Vadim Sokolov, Picture Perfect, USA; **curly** Zviki-Eshet, The Stock Market; **dam** Mark E. Gibson, The Stock Market; **dentist** © 2003 PhotoDisc, Inc./Getty Images; **desert** J. Ramey, Stockphotos; **dig** Bob Daemmrich, The Image Works; **dive** David Stoecklein, The Stock Market; **dock** David A. Cantor, The Stock Market; **doctor** Robert Frerck, The Stock Market; **dog** Kevin Morris, Allstock; **donkey** Kevin Schafer, Allstock; **dress** Nancy Brown, The Image Bank; **dry** Terje Rakke, The Image Bank; **duck** John Cancalosi, Stock, Boston; **eagle** Tom Walker, Allstock; **earth** NASA/Mark Marten, Photo Researchers, Inc.; **eat** Phoebe Ferguson; **edge** Larry Kolvoord, The Image Works; **elbow** Rosanne Olson, Allstock; **elephant** Alan Briere, SuperStock; **engineer** Frank Siteman, Stock, Boston; **enter** Mary Kate Denny, PhotoEdit; **evening** David G. Toerge, Black Star; **exciting** Charles Krebs, Allstock; **exercise** Tim Davis, Allstock; **explore** Larry Kolvoord, The Image Works; **fair** Index Stock International; **fall** Sandy Clark, The Stock Market; **far** Scott Smith, Picture Perfect, USA; **farm** Mitch Wojnarowicz, The Image Works; **feed** Jim Pickerell, Stock, Boston; **fence** Paul G. Elson, The Image Bank; **field** Bohdan Hrynewych, Stock, Boston; **fireplace** Patti McConville, The Image Bank; **fireworks** P.F. Bentley, Black Star; **fish** David Hall, The Image Works; **fisherman** Glenn Oakley, Black Star; **flag** Dieter Menne, The Image Bank; **flock** Eastcott/Momatiuk, The Image Works; **flood** Shelly Katz, Black Star; **flower** Art Wolfe, Allstock; **fly** Lorraine Rorke, The Image Works; **fog** C. Hotchkiss, Photo Researchers, Inc.; **football** David Madison, Duomo Photography; **forest** Frans Lanting, Minden Pictures; **fossil** F. Thomas, SuperStock; **fox** Tom Edwards, Animals, Animals; **friend** Richard Hutchings, Photo Researchers, Inc.; **frog** James H. Carmichael, Jr., The Image Bank; **frost** SuperStock; **funny** Erik Leigh Simmons, The Image Bank; **furniture** Picture Perfect, USA; **garage** M. Hayman, Photo Researchers, Inc.; **garden** Larry Lefever, Grant Heilman Photography; **gate** David Morris, Midwestock; **giraffe** Martin Harvey, The Wildlife Collection; **glass** David de Lossey, The Image Bank; **goat** Larry Lefever, Grant Heilman Photography; **goose** Giuliano Colliva, The Image Bank; **grass** John Colwell, Grant Heilman Photography; **greenhouse** Oddo and Sinibaldi, The Stock Market; **grin** SuperStock; **group** Karen Preuss, The Image Works; **guard** Garry Gay, The Image Bank; **gym** Bob Daemmrich, The Image Works; **haircut** Richard Hutchings, PhotoEdit; **Halloween** Lee F. Snyder, Photo Researchers, Inc.; **hamster** Joe Deveney, The Image Bank; **hang** Paul Hurd, Allstock; **hatch** Frans Lanting, Minden Pictures; **hawk** Fernando Bergamaschi, The Image Bank; **head** Lawrence Migdale, Stock, Boston; **helicopter** Joe Azzara, The Image Bank; **hen** Larry Lefever, Grant Heilman Photography; **hill** Roy Bishop, Stock, Boston; **hippopotamus** Walt Anderson, Visuals Unlimited; **hockey** Pool, Gamma Liaison; **hole** Alan Carey, The Image Works; **hop** David Barnes, Allstock; **horn** Francois Gohier, Allstock; **house** Gay Bumgarner, Tony Stone Images; **hug** Bob Daemmrich, Stock, Boston; **hump** Leonard Rue, Stock, Boston; **hut** Lionel Isy-Schwart, The Image Bank; **igloo** David A. Rosenberg, Allstock;

inside Jean Pierre Pieuchot, The Image Bank; **instrument** Bob Daemmrich, The Image Works; **island** Guido Alberto Rossi, The Image Bank; **jellyfish** Breck P. Kent, Animals, Animals; **jet** Gary Gladstone, The Image Bank; **jog** Donald Graham, Index Stock Photography; **judge** Michal Heron, Woodfin Camp & Associates; **juggle** B & J McGrath, The Picture Cube; **jump** Renee Lynn, Photo Researchers, Inc.; **jungle** Gary Braasch, Allstock; **junk** Mark Antman, The Image Works; **kangaroo** Stephanie Stokes, The Stock Market; **kick** David Stoeklein, Allstock; **kitchen** David Frazier, The Stock Market; **kitten** Robert Pearcy, Animals, Animals; **lake** David Muench, Allstock; **lamb** Jon Davison, Stockphotos; **laundry** Jon Lamar, The Stock Market; **lead²** Bruce Wellman, Stock, Boston; **leaf** Rich Iwasaki, Allstock; **leather** Kory Addis, The Picture Cube; **leg** Bob Daemmrich, Stock, Boston; **library** Bob Daemmrich, Stock, Boston; **lift** Michael Newman, PhotoEdit; **lighthouse** Chad Elers, Allstock; **lightning** Barry L. Runk, Grant Heilman Photography; **lion** Michael Dick, Animals, Animals; **lip** Lawrence Migdale, Stock, Boston; **load** John Coletti, The Picture Cube; **lobster** Andrew Martinez, Photo Researchers, Inc.; **log** William Johnson, Stock, Boston; **machine** John Greenleigh, Apple Computer; **maple** John Serrao, Photo Researchers, Inc.; **march** Steve Stone, The Picture Cube; **marsh** Richard Hamilton Smith, Allstock; **mask** Phoebe Ferguson; **meadow** T. Leeson, Photo Researchers, Inc.; **melt** Gary E. Holscher, Allstock; **microscope** Matthew Jordan Smith; **mirror** Lawrence Migdale, Stock, Boston; **model** A. Boccaccio, The Image Bank; **money** Bob Daemmrich, Stock, Boston; **monkey** Gerard Lacz, Peter Arnold, Inc.; **moon** Peter Menzel, Photo Researchers, Inc.; **morning** William Johnson, Stock, Boston; **moth** J.H. Robinson, Photo Researchers, Inc.; **motorcycle** John Kane, Stockphotos; **mountain** Darrell Gulin, Allstock; **mud** J. Gerard Smith, Photo Researchers, Inc.; **narrow** Eric Berndt, Midwestock; **neighbor** Catherine Karnow, Woodfin Camp & Associates; **newspaper** David Woods, The Stock Market; **night** EyeWire/Getty Images; **nose** Ken Straiton, The Stock Market; **nurse** Goivaux Communications, Phototake. NYC; **ocean** SuperStock; **office** Chuck Keeler, Tony Stone Images; **oil** Ben Gibson/Katz Pictures/Woodfin Camp & Associates; **orchestra** David J. Maenza, The Image Bank; **oven** Stephen W. Frisch, Stock, Boston; **owl** Roy Morsch, The Stock Market; **paint** Don Mason, The Stock Market; **parade** Joan Baron, The Stock Market; **park** John Banagan, The Image Bank; **party** Fiona Pragoff, Stockphotos; **paw** Margot Conte, Animals, Animals; **penguin** Frans Lanting, Minden Pictures; **phone** EyeWire/Getty Images; **piano** Bob Daemmrich, The Image Works; **picnic** Roger & Donna Aitkenhead, Earth Scenes; **pig** Zig Leszczynski, Animals, Animals; **pipe** Anchorage Daily News, Gamma Liaison; **plant** Ryan Beyer, Allstock; **playground** Michael Salas, The Image Bank; **point** Bob Daemmrich, The Image Works; **pole** Frank P. Rossotto, The Stock Market; **pony** Michael Habicht, Animals, Animals; **present** Gabe Palmer, The Stock Market; **prize** James Holland, Stock, Boston; **propeller** Larry Downing, Woodfin Camp & Associates; **puddle** Andre Gallant, The Image Bank; **puppy** Laura Dwight, Peter Arnold, Inc.; **race** Arthur Grace, Stock, Boston; **raft** R. Llewellyn, SuperStock; **rainbow** John M. Roberts, The Stock Market; **read** Gene Dwiggins, Black Star; **rhinoceros** Art Wolfe, Allstock; **ride** Richard Kolar, Earth Scenes; **ring** Paul Gerda, Leo De Wys, Inc.; **river** Pat O'Hara, Allstock; **road** Joe Sohm, The Image Works; **robin** Charles Mann, Photo Researchers, Inc.; **rocket** NASA; **roof** Harald Sund, The Image Bank; **rooster** Robert Maier, Animals, Animals; **rope** Allen Bragdon, The Image Bank; **rose** John Livzey, Allstock; **run** Victoria Beller-Smith; **sail** Joe Towers, The Stock Market; **sand** Picture Perfect, USA; **saw** Paul Loven, Picture Perfect, USA; **scarecrow** Peter Miller, The Image Bank; **school** Frank Siteman, The Picture Cube; **scientist** Peter Saloutos, The Stock Market; **seat** Joseph Nettis, Stock, Boston; **seed** Index Stock International; **seesaw** Alan Carey, The Image Works; **sheep** W. & D. McIntyre, Photo Researchers, Inc.; **short** Myrleen Ferguson, PhotoEdit; **sidewalk** Thomas Fletcher, Stock, Boston; **sign** Tom McHugh, Photo Researchers, Inc.; **sit** Jim Cummins, Allstock; **ski** J.F. Causse, Tony Stone Images; **smile** John Livzey, Allstock; **snow** Jean Pierre Pieuchot, The Image Bank; **soccer** Rick Friedman, Black Star; **soil** Bob Daemmrich, Stock, Boston; **spell** Nancy Sheehan, The Picture Cube; **spot** Camerique, H. Armstrong Roberts; **stair** Brett Froomer, The Image Bank; **station** Joe Azzara, The Image Bank; **statue** Peter Saloutos, The Stock Market; **steel** Ben Simmons, The Stock Market; **stick** Roy Morsch, The Stock Market; **store** Andy Caulfield, The Image Bank; **storm** Kjell B. Sandved, Visuals Unlimited; **stove** David Young-Wolff, PhotoEdit; **street** J & M Ibbotson, Allstock; **submarine** J. Urwiller, H. Armstrong Roberts; **suds** Peter L. Chapman, Stock, Boston; **suit** Tim Brown, Tony Stone Images; **supermarket** Lou Jones, The Image Bank; **surface** Oli Tennent, Tony Stone Images; **swamp** Luis Castaneda, The Image Bank; **swim** Kirk Schlea, Picture Perfect, USA; **tail** Warren Jacobi, Picture Perfect, USA; **tall** EyeWire/Getty Images; **taxi** Donald Graham, Allstock; **team** Jeff Smith, The Image Bank; **teeth** Jeff Persons, Stock, Boston; **telephone** J. Gerard Smith, Photo Researchers, Inc.; **telescope** Bob Daemmrich, The Image Works; **tennis** LaFoto, H. Armstrong Roberts; **theater** Wayne Eastep, The Stock Market; **throw** Roy Morsch, The Stock Market; **tiger** Charles Mahaux, The Image Bank; **tongue** Joan Teasdale, The Stock Market; **tornado** E.R. Degginger, Earth Scenes; **tractor** David Barnes, The Stock Market; **trailer** Lionel Delevingne, Stock, Boston; **train** Stan Ries, Leo De Wys, Inc.; **trash** Barbara Alper, Stock, Boston; **truck** R. King, SuperStock; **tube** Erika Stone, Peter Arnold, Inc.; **tunnel** David Sailors, The Stock Market; **turkey** Vince Streano, Allstock; **underwater** Stephen Frink, Allstock; **uniform** SuperStock; **up** Bob Daemmrich, Stock, Boston; **valley** Bud Lehnhausen, Photo Researchers, Inc.; **village** John Elk, Stock, Boston; **wagon** Jim Pickerell, Stock, Boston; **walk** B. Bachmann, Allstock; **wall** Peter Miller, The Image Bank; **wash** Laimute Druskis, Stock, Boston; **wave** Arthur Grace, Stock, Boston; **web** Roy Morsch, The Stock Market; **weigh** Joseph Nettis, Photo Researchers, Inc.; **wet** John Lei, Stock, Boston; **wild** Jim Stamates, Allstock; **win** Kaz Mori, The Image Bank; **wire** Tony Freeman, PhotoEdit; **wolf** Zig Leszczynski, Animals, Animals; **wool** Roy Attaway, Photo Researchers, Inc.; **wrinkle** Robert Pearcy, Animals Animals; **yard** Jeff Hunter, The Image Bank; **yawn** R. Hutchings, Photo Researchers, Inc.; **young** Benn Mitchell, The Image Bank; **zebra** Leonard Lee Rue III, Photo Researchers, Inc.